CUSTOMIZED INTERNATIONAL INVESTMENT DECISIONS

Sedef Uncu Akı

CUSTOMIZED INTERNATIONAL INVESTMENT DECISIONS

AN EXPLORATION INTO THE TEXTILE AND APPAREL DECISION-MAKING PROCESS

VDM Verlag Dr. Müller

Impressum/Imprint (nur für Deutschland/ only for Germany)
Bibliografische Information der Deutschen Nationalbibliothek: Die Deutsche Nationalbibliothek
verzeichnet diese Publikation in der Deutschen Nationalbibliografie; detaillierte bibliografische
Daten sind im Internet über http://dnb.d-nb.de abrufbar.
Alle in diesem Buch genannten Marken und Produktnamen unterliegen warenzeichen-, marken-
oder patentrechtlichem Schutz bzw. sind Warenzeichen oder eingetragene Warenzeichen der
jeweiligen Inhaber. Die Wiedergabe von Marken, Produktnamen, Gebrauchsnamen,
Handelsnamen, Warenbezeichnungen u.s.w. in diesem Werk berechtigt auch ohne besondere
Kennzeichnung nicht zu der Annahme, dass solche Namen im Sinne der Warenzeichen- und
Markenschutzgesetzgebung als frei zu betrachten wären und daher von jedermann benutzt
werden dürften.

Coverbild: www.purestockx.com

Verlag: VDM Verlag Dr. Müller Aktiengesellschaft & Co. KG
Dudweiler Landstr. 99, 66123 Saarbrücken, Deutschland
Telefon +49 681 9100-698, Telefax +49 681 9100-988, Email: info@vdm-verlag.de
Zugl.: Raleigh, North Carolina State University, Dissertation, 2003

Herstellung in Deutschland:
Schaltungsdienst Lange o.H.G., Berlin
Books on Demand GmbH, Norderstedt
Reha GmbH, Saarbrücken
Amazon Distribution GmbH, Leipzig
ISBN: 978-3-639-16134-2

Imprint (only for USA, GB)
Bibliographic information published by the Deutsche Nationalbibliothek: The Deutsche
Nationalbibliothek lists this publication in the Deutsche Nationalbibliografie; detailed
bibliographic data are available in the Internet at http://dnb.d-nb.de.
Any brand names and product names mentioned in this book are subject to trademark, brand or
patent protection and are trademarks or registered trademarks of their respective holders. The use
of brand names, product names, common names, trade names, product descriptions etc. even
without a particular marking in this works is in no way to be construed to mean that such names
may be regarded as unrestricted in respect of trademark and brand protection legislation and
could thus be used by anyone.

Cover image: www.purestockx.com

Publisher:
VDM Verlag Dr. Müller Aktiengesellschaft & Co. KG
Dudweiler Landstr. 99, 66123 Saarbrücken, Germany
Phone +49 681 9100-698, Fax +49 681 9100-988, Email: info@vdm-publishing.com
Raleigh, North Carolina State University, Dissertation, 2003

Printed in the U.S.A.
Printed in the U.K. by (see last page)
ISBN: 978-3-639-16134-2

TABLE OF CONTENTS

2

4

PART I: INTRODUCTION

In an interconnected world economy, the new challenge for companies is the ability to see the entire world as the playing field. Today, the ideal global corporation exploits every new opportunity in the environment, controls every threat that may occur, and creates effective strategies to stay competitive. Companies try to have a favorable presence in the right place at the right time. A failure in the effort to find the right choice can be quite costly for them. Since this type of decision directly influences the basic motivations of corporate strategy, like growth, profits and security, by gaining access to new markets or sources of supply.

Favorable presence is defined for this study as *investing globally for production*. This investment can be actualized in three ways: greenfield operations[1], strategic partnerships, and sourcing. Companies locate production abroad to utilize the comparative advantages among different countries (Camuffo, Romano, & Vinelli, 2001; Dunning, 1988; Murray & Kotabe, 1999). Research on international production has revealed that there are advantages deriving from asset ownership (e.g., tangible assets, patents, technology, skills), location-bound endowments (e.g., unit prices and quality, investment incentives, infrastructure, culture, and trade barriers), and internationalization of cross-border market transactions (Brush, Maritan, & Karnani, 1999; Dunning, 1988).

Companies often try to exploit their competitive advantage by using the comparative advantage of geographical differences. However, this process requires a tremendous amount of effort and capital. In addition, there always exists the possibility of ultimate failure due to long term and short term uncertainty in the environment. Many

---

[1] "Greenfield operations" refers to buying or building plants in a location. Companies have 100% ownership of the greenfield operation.

7

American companies fail to realize the full potential of their foreign investments and Hoch (1982) argues that faulty location selection is the major cause for this shortfall.

Today, the failure of investment decisions has contributed to the struggle that US textile and apparel companies have faced. Patterns of global production and trade have changed after several major agreements for the US Textile and Apparel industry. These changes were ignited in 1994 with North American Free Trade Agreement (NAFTA) and exploded with Caribbean Basin Trade Partnership Act (CBTPA), the African Growth and Opportunity Act (AGOA) and other special agreements with mostly developing countries. For example, some of the leading textile companies started to invest mostly in Mexico to strengthen their positions in the North American region. "Given the present trade and consumer environment, either we play the game by looking at the most cost-effective way of production, or we go out of business," said John Bakane, Cone Mills chief executive (Burritt, 2000). In a newspaper article, a Duke University sociologist said "The headquarters of these global companies are very likely to stay in the United States, but I think a lot of the production side is likely to continue going south" (Burritt, 2000).

Newspapers have published striking articles, which discussed the failure of the leading textile companies in Mexico. One of the comments was in the News & Record "On an otherwise empty plot of land in eastern Mexico sits what some are calling Guilford Mills' $40 million failure." in the News & Record (Heisler, 2003). The article continues with;

> "The now shuttered textile factory was part of a larger plan in the late 1990s to take advantage of North American Free Trade Agreement and save the company from low-cost Asian rivals. Instead, the plant, built in Altamira, fell victim to miscalculations and global economic changes." (Heisler, 2003)

Projects[2] that have failed are:

- Burlington Industries' jeans joint venture in Chihuahua, with an estimated loss of $20 million according to bankruptcy court documents.

---

[2] This list is modified by the author from the newspaper article of Heisler, 2003.

- An industrial park in the state of Morelos by Guilford, Burlington and others' cooperation. It failed after it was hampered with labor problems. (Combined losses in excess of $25 million)
- Guilford's Altamira fabric plant with an estimated loss of $40 million.

Reasons for these failures may be 'miscalculations' as stated in the article, or economic changes that influenced Mexico's position and turned it to a more difficult place to do business. Some people assert that the leading textile companies did not have a well-conceived plan considering every aspect of the investment decision. "They failed to realize that the Mexican culture is different from what we're used to." said John Schmonsees, a senior trade specialist with the U.S. Dept. of Commerce (Heisler, 2003).

In addition to the happenings in Mexico, other trade agreements were signed with countries. Central American countries with Caribbean Basin Trade Partnership Act (CBTPA) and African countries with the African Growth and Opportunity Act (AGOA) have gained new advantages for producing goods for the US market. These changing dynamics also affected Mexico's former advantage for the US.

Some companies have preferred not making the move to Mexico. Craig Crockard, vice president of Avondale Mills, said "Just because the labor is cheaper does not make it better," Since 1997, the Monroe (NC)-based company has invested more than $150 million in its fabric mills in South Carolina and Alabama. "We think we can be competitive here." In addition, some executives had doubts about the quality of fabrics, the electricity interruptions and the hijacking of trucks in Mexico (Burritt, 2000).

The decision to manufacture in the US is always considered in terms of it being the right decision or not. Definitely, the failures in Mexico showed that they lacked a structured decision-making methodology for international investments. Thus, they may not have had the opportunity to analyze the decisions thoroughly and may have overlooked critical parts. However, it is also clear that staying in the US is not the right solution for all types of the textile companies. The discussion of finding the right investment reveals the need for an investigation about international investment

9

decisions. In the literature, different methodologies from various research areas have been developed to solve these complex problems (Schniederjans, 1999). However, there are specific assumptions and limited coverage of the plant location problem according to each area's interest. Economists, for example, try to optimize the allocation of resources by means of theoretical reasoning. Industrial geographers, on the other hand, blend economics with geography for the formulation of new industrial developments. Management people examine the problem, mostly, from a strategic point of view. A considerable number of researchers have conducted empirical studies to determine the important location factors for different industry segments. Engineers have developed the most sophisticated mathematical analyses; however, it is hard for these types of models to include the important factors that cannot be quantified.

The models used by researchers vary from basic, easy to apply models like scaling, scoring, ranking, to highly complex and hard to develop models like heuristic algorithms and simulations. Each modeling technique has its own advantages and disadvantages. Companies have to select the most appropriate model that can serve their needs properly.

In conclusion, due to changing market dynamics, companies are forced to consider macro-environmental factors including economic, social, political, legal, technological factors, and micro-environmental factors including customers, competitors, and suppliers. Global competition will be tougher with the elimination of quotas by 2005. Under these circumstances, there is a need for the textile and apparel industry to develop a model that is all-inclusive for the international investment decisions yet allows effective decision-making.

The proposed conceptual model is shown in Figure 1. This model considers both:

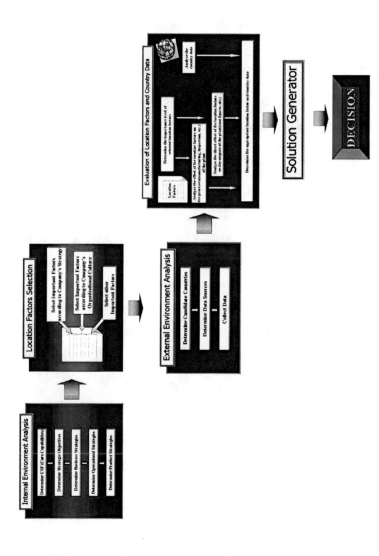

Figure 1 Proposed conceptual model for international investment decisions

6

o the internal environment of the company by questioning the strategic approach and the organizational culture of the company, and

o the external environment of the company by considering the important location factors.

This model is going to be questioned under the following research purposes.

RESEARCH PURPOSES

The purposes of this research are to develop:

- A taxonomy of existing methodologies for plant location investment decisions.

- A comprehensive instrument for investment decisions considering the strategy of the company, the organizational culture of the company, the sector where the company operates, and the role of external environment.

- A structured decision-making model for customized international investment decisions, considering companies in different sectors, which pursue different strategies and have different organizational cultures.

- A decision support tool based on the above conceptual model, which incorporates both the quantitative and the qualitative factors to provide an all-inclusive model to the decision maker.

RESEARCH OBJECTIVES

After reviewing the literature, this research aims to:

- Determine a comprehensive "international investment location factors list" and categorize these factors based on the strategy, organizational culture and sector of the company.

- Develop a conceptual model for international plant location analysis, which considers both:

o the internal environment of the company by questioning the strategic approach organizational culture, and sector type of the company, and o the external environment of the company by considering the location factors that are specific for different countries.

- Determine data sources for international investment decisions
- Develop a new interpretation to quantify the qualitative factors.
- Develop a decision support tool, which helps analyze the proposed plant considering both the quantitative factors and the qualitative factors (such as the strategic concerns, the operational concerns, and the environmental concerns), of the company.

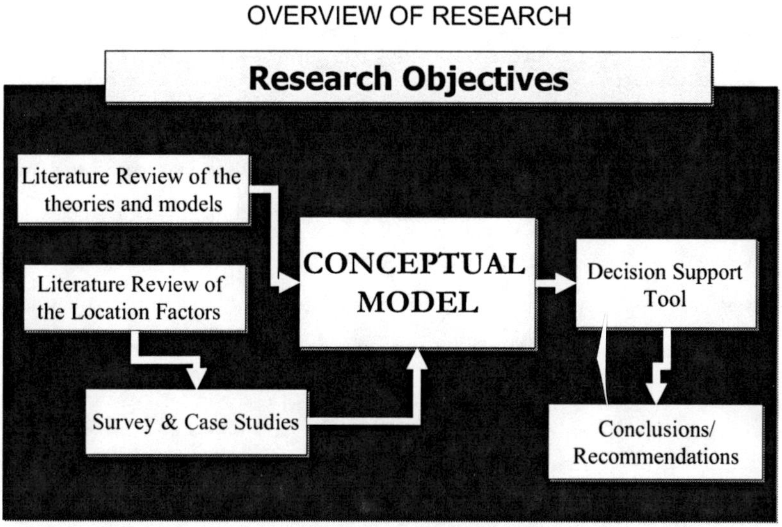

OVERVIEW OF RESEARCH

Figure 2 Graphical depiction of research methodology

After identifying the research objectives, a research methodology was developed to clarify the path to satisfy the objectives (Figure 2). In this methodology, there were five steps:

1. Literature Review
2. Survey and Case Studies

3. Conceptual Model

4. A Decision Support Tool

5. Conclusions/Recommendations

The first step was the review of the existing plant location literature. This review was performed to identify the need for an additional research about this topic, and to collect information for development of the conceptual model and the survey instrument.

The second step was the survey and case study application. With the inputs from the literature, a survey instrument was developed to collect data from the fiber, textile, apparel, and nonwoven companies. Survey results are elaborated with specific case studies. The details of this step are discussed in Part V.

Conceptual model development was the third step in this research. This model aimed to enhance the existing studies and to close the gaps in the literature. Findings from the literature review and survey and case study analyses are incorporated into the conceptual model. Validation of the model was conducted during the case studies.

At the fourth step, a decision support tool was developed based on the conceptual model. This tool can be used to generate actual results for decision makers. Details will be discussed in Part VI. The last step was the integrated conclusions and the recommendations section.

Significance of the Study

There exist four significant aspects of this study.

1. Location factors will be classified based on the strategic approach of US textile and apparel industries after analyzing the results of the developed survey. Empirical research exists on the classification of the factors. However, none of the studies incorporated the strategic approach of the firm.

2. A structured multi-criteria decision-making model which allows customization is developed using the findings of the survey and case studies.

14

3. During the model generation, data sources related to the international investment decisions are compiled.

4. Methods to quantify the qualitative data are generated during the data collection phase for the decision support tool.

These last two aspects serve the purpose of incorporating both the quantitative and the qualitative data into the model. Results from this study will assist to the US textile and apparel companies in a way that they will be able to analyze the projected investment locations effectively, considering all characteristics of location factors mentioned above.

Justification of the Study

A search for location factors specific to the textile and apparel industry was conducted; however, there was limited literature. The aim of this study is to contribute to the body of knowledge by providing appropriate literature for studying the location factors for this industry.

Limitations of the Study

There are three limitations of this study:

- The survey and case study research were conducted with a limited sample. Thus, the results of the survey and the case studies may not be representative of all textile and apparel companies.

- Every variable was considered as independent. However, there are clear interactions (correlations) that are beyond the scope of this study.

- Although sourcing is included in the definition of international investments, the focus of the literature review was primarily on the advanced stages of international investments (i.e., greenfield operations and strategic partnerships).

15

ORGANIZATION

This dissertation first presents the literature review of the investment decisions. The literature review section is covered in Part II and Part III. In Part II, different methodologies for investment decision are analyzed. The limitations and advantages of each methodology are analyzed according to the characteristics of international plant location decisions so that the decision makers can select the appropriate method for their organizations. Part II was presented at IFFTI conference in Hong Kong in November, 2002 (Uncu, Hodge, Oxenham, & Jones, 2002).

Part III of the dissertation reviews the literature related to the different location factors that have been considered from 1909 to today. Factors are analyzed according to the different historical periods. The evolution of the location factors is discussed and a comprehensive list of location factors was formed for international investment decisions. This list is used in the 'Customized Investment Decisions Tool' in Part IV.

The paper given in the Part IV of this dissertation provides a customized investment decisions tool for companies. This instrument was developed to guide the companies to an effective combination of the location factors and their priorities according to companies' specific needs.

This tool is then used to conduct an empirical analysis of the companies in US Textile and Apparel Industry, which is presented in Part V of the dissertation. Survey and case studies are used as the research methodology for this paper. Results are discussed and are incorporated into Part VI of this dissertation.

Part VI is the conceptual framework for international investment analysis. Data that come from the literature review (Part II & Part III) and the empirical analysis (Part V) were analyzed and a conceptual model was developed for customized international investment decisions.

In Part VII, a decision support tool was developed using the conceptual model (Part VI). Microsoft Access® is used as the software for this tool. International data sources are found during the development stage of this decision support tool. Finally, the conclusions of this study and recommendations are presented in Part VIII.

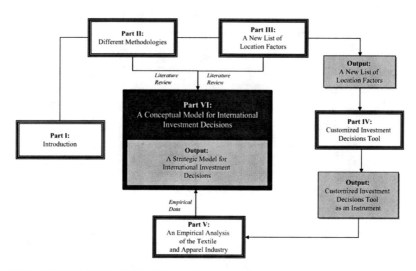

Figure 3 Organization of the dissertation

The organization of the dissertation is summarized in Figure 3. Each part has its own reference list and appendices. Numbering of tables and figures is consecutive in the entire document. One list of tables and one list of figures are presented at the beginning of the dissertation in a cumulative form including each section's figures and tables.

Definition of Terms

Terms are defined throughout the document due to the organization. Table 1 shows the parts of the document and the page numbers where the specified terms are defined.

Table 1 Definition of terms

Term	Part
Greenfield Operations	Part I, pg.2
Location Factors	Part III, pg.56
Total Cost of Product	Part III, pg.66
Cost of Quota	Part III, pg.66
Tax Rate	Part III, pg.62
Transaction Costs	Part III, pg.67
Participation in Economic Trade Groups	Part III, pg.67
Cost of Land	Part III, pg.67
Government Incentives	Part III, pg.67
Availability of Skilled Labor	Part III, pg.68
Bargaining Power of Suppliers	Part III, pg.68
Availability of Lending Institutions	Part III, pg.68
Availability of Middle Management	Part III, pg.69
Lead Time	Part III, pg.69
Flexibility of Production	Part III, pg.69
Political Stability	Part III, pg.70
Banking System Stability	Part III, pg.71
National Content Laws Countries	Part III, pg.71
Clarity of Corporate Investment Rules	Part III, pg.72
Internal Environment of the Company	Part IV, pg.85
Comparative Advantage	Part IV, pg.85
Competitive Advantage	Part IV, pg.85
Organizational Culture	Part IV, pg.86
Sector of the Company	Part IV, pg.88
External Environment of the Company	Part IV, pg.89

REFERENCES

Brimberg, J., & ReVelle, C. (1999). A multi-facility location model with partial satisfaction of demand. Studies in Locational Analysis, 13, 91-101.

Brimberg, J., & ReVelle, C. (2000). The maximum return-on-investment plant location. Journal of the Operational Research Society, 51, 729-735.

Badri, M. A. (1999). Combining the Analytic Hierarchy Process and Goal Programming for Global Facility Location-Allocation Problem. International Journal of Production Economics, 62, 237-248

Brush, T. H., Maritan, C. A., & Karnani, A. (1999). The Plant Location Decision in Multinational Manufacturing Firms: An Empirical Analysis of International Business and Manufacturing Strategy Perspectives. Production and Operations Management, 8(2), 109-132.

Burritt, C. (Dec 17, 2000). Seven years into NAFTA, textile makers seek payoff in Mexico\Textiles: Payoff Sought in Mexico. The Atlanta Journal-Constitution.

Camuffo, A., Romano, P., & Vinelli, A. (2001). Back to the future: Benetton transforms its global network. MIT Sloan Management Review (Fall), 46-52.

Canel, C., & Das, S., R. (2002). Modeling Global Facility Location Decisions:Integrating Marketing and Manufacturing Decisions. Industrial Management & Data Systems, 102(2), 110-118.

Canel, C., & Khumawala, B. M. (1997). Multi-period international facilities location:an algorithm and application. International Journal of Production Research, 35(7), 1891-1910.

Chakravarty, A. K. (1999). Profit margin, process improvement and capacity decisions in global manufacturing. International Journal of Production Research, 37(18), 4235-4257.

Chuang, P. T. (2001). Combining the Analytical Hierarchy Process and Quality Function Deployment for a Location Decision from a Requirement Perspective. The International Journal of Advanced Manufacturing Technology, 18, 842-849.

Current, J., Ratick, S., & ReVelle, C. (1997). Dynamic Facility Location When the Total Number of Facilities is Uncertain: A Decision Analysis Approach. European Journal of Operational Research, 110, 597-609.

Dunning, J. H. (1988). The Eclectic Paradigm of International Production: A Restatement and Some Possible Extensions. Journal of International Business Studies(Spring), 1-31.

Heisler, E. (March 16, 2003). Struggle: South of the border; the textile experiment in Mexico showed promise, but problems piled up quickly. Ultimately, corporate mistakes and economic misfortunes led to failures. The News & Record.

Hoch, L. C. (1982). Site Selection for Foreign Operations. Industrial Development, 151, 7-9.

Holmberg, K., Ronnqvist, M., & Yuan, D. (1999). An Exact Algorithm for the Capacitated Facility Location Problems with Single Sourcing. European Journal of Operational Research, 113(3), 544-559.

Houshyar, A., & White, B. (1997). Comparison of Solution Procedures to the Facility Location Problem. Computers and Industrial Engineering, 32(1), 77-87.

Lim, S. K., & Kim, Y. D. (1999). An Integrated Approach to Dynamic Plant Loation and Capacity Planning. Journal of the Operational Research Society, 50, 1205-1216. Owen, S. H., & Daskin, M. S. (1998). Strategic Facility Location: A Review. European Journal of Operational Research, 111, 423-447.

Murray, J. Y., & Kotabe, M. (1999). Sourcing strategies of US Service companies: A modified transaction cost analysis. Strategic Management Journal, 20, 791-809.

Saaty, T. L. (1988). Multicriteria Decision Making: The Analytic Hierarchy Process. United States.

Schmidt, G., & Wilhelm, W. E. (2000). Strategic, tactical and operational decisions in multi-national logistics networks: a review and discussion of modeling issues. International Journal of Production Research, 38(7), 1501-1523.

Schniederjans, M. J. (1999). International Facility Acquisition and Location Analysis. London: Quorum Books.

Tombak, M. M. (1995). Multinational Plant Location as a Game of Timing. European Journal of Operational Research, 86, 434-451.

Uncu, S., Hodge, G. L., Oxenham, W., & Jones, M. R. (2002). An Analysis of Current Methodologies for International Plant Location Decisions. Paper presented at the IIFFTI, Hong Kong Polytechnic University, Hong Kong.

PART II: AN ANALYSIS OF THE CURRENT METHODOLOGIES FOR INTERNATIONAL PLANT LOCATION SELECTION

Published in: IFFTI Conference
7-9 November, 2002
Hong Kong

Uncu, S., Hodge, G. L., Oxenham, W., & Jones, M. R. (2002). *An Analysis of Current Methodologies for International Plant Location Decisions.* Paper presented at the IFFTI, Hong Kong Polytechnic University, Hong Kong

AN ANALYSIS OF THE CURRENT METHODOLOGIES FOR

INTERNATIONAL PLANT LOCATION SELECTION

S. Uncu, G. Hodge, W. Oxenham, M. Jones

North Carolina State University, Raleigh, NC, USA

ABSTRACT

As competition evolves, new dynamics of the global economy unfold. To cope with these changing dynamics, companies are taking strategic actions to sustain their competitive advantages. Internationalization of an organization is an important strategic action in this respect since it has a direct effect on meeting the basic motivations of a company's corporate strategy (growth, profits and security) by gaining access to new markets or sources of supply.

Today, many companies make decisions on international location. In recent history, however, many of them either have ceased their international operations or failed to realize the full potential of their international investments due to failure in international location selection.

This paper examines the current methodologies for international plant location selections. These methodologies include scaling, scoring, ranking methods, analytic hierarchy process (AHP) methodology, mathematical programming methods, heuristic algorithms and simulation methods. The limitations and advantages of each methodology are analyzed according to the characteristics of international plant location decisions so that the decision makers can find the appropriate method for their organizations. In the current climate of rapid internationalization, this paper serves as a guide to international plant location decision-making.

Keywords: International plant location, decision making, AHP, mathematical programming, heuristic algorithms, simulation

INTRODUCTION

Plant location studies formally started in 1909 when Alfred Weber investigated

the problem of how to position a single warehouse so as to minimize the total distance

between the warehouse and several customers (Owen & Daskin, 1998). However,

workable and realistic models and algorithms emerged only in the mid-1960s with the arrival of computers (ReVelle & Laporte, 1996). Since then, several models and algorithms have been developed to solve specific plant location problems.

Until recently, the scope of the plant location problem was limited. Only locations in the same country were taken into consideration. Yet, market dynamics have changed due to globalization. In 1986, McDonald (1986) put forth the concept of a 'floating' factory to prove these rapid changes taking place around the globe (Canel & Khumawala, 1997). He argues that factories should take the shape of a floating factory which is ready to move to an economic opportunity. If it does not act, it loses its markets to competitors (McDonald, 1986). So, the attention has inevitably evolved into the international arena. This evolution has also changed the characteristics of the decision making for plant locations. New factors, such as exchange rates, labor costs, government incentives, etc. have entered into consideration. With this expansion, the complexity of the problem has increased vastly. Today, a plant location decision is a long-term strategic decision for a company to satisfy multiple objectives based on both quantitative and qualitative criteria.

Various plant location decision models have been developed to select the appropriate

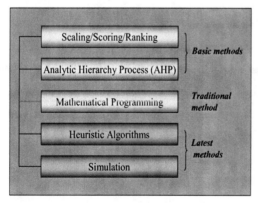

location through analyzing a choice of location factors (Yang & Lee, 1997). For textile and apparel industry, international plant location decisions are complex due to numerous location factors that have increased after the trade agreements including NAFTA, GATT and CBI.

Figure 4 Current methodologies for international plant location decisions

Due to changing market dynamics, companies are forced to consider elaborately macro environment factors including economic, social, political, legal, technological factors, and microenvironment factors including customers, competitors, and suppliers. Under these circumstances, the challenge for textile and apparel industry is to determine a model that is all inclusive yet allows effective decision making.

This paper identifies several different methodologies for international plant location selection. Basic scaling, scoring, ranking methodologies, traditional mathematical programming methodologies, and the latest solution methodologies (such as heuristic algorithms and simulation), are taken into consideration. A detailed analysis is conducted for each methodology. Advantages and disadvantages of the methods are investigated considering the characteristics of international plant location decisions. In the current climate of rapid internationalization, this paper serves as a guide to international plant location decision-making.

CHARACTERISTICS OF INTERNATIONAL PLANT LOCATION DECISIONS

An accurate analysis of the existing methodologies can only be conducted if the characteristics of international plant location decisions are well recognized. In the light of this fact, these characteristics will be examined before proceeding to the existing methodologies. Basically, international plant location decisions have three major characteristics. They are multilevel decisions, multi-criteria decisions and multi periodic decisions.

Multilevel Decisions

There exist three levels in international plant location decision-making (Figure 5). The first level is the strategic level. It includes the selection of the right country. (e.g. South Africa, Mexico, China). The second level is the tactical level, which represents the selection of the region within the country, such as the east coast or the west coast of China. The last level is the operational level. Appropriate site selection is the aim in this level. An appropriate site in the east coast of China which is near to the port may be the decision at the operational level.

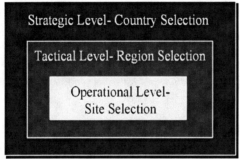

Strategic Level- Country Selection

Tactical Level- Region Selection

Operational Level-
Site Selection

Figure 5 Different levels of international plant location decisions

Multi-Criteria Decisions

In classical location theory, the crucial factors for plant locations are transportation, costs of materials and labor costs (Yurimoto & Masui, 1995). However, in the case of international plant location decisions, not only are the cost and profit factors critical criteria for the decision, but economic, social, and political factors also play a crucial role. Besides, as the level of decision changes from country level to tactical level or from tactical level to operational level, different criteria appear under the same generic criterion such as labor, transportation, economic factors, political factors, etc. For example, availability of transportation can be a critical factor in the strategic level, however, in the tactical level, this factor may become the quality of transportation and for operational level, number of highways, rail roads, etc. may be the important factor for the generic transportation criterion.

Multi-periodic Decisions

The key factors may change over time in today's dynamic environment (Yang & Lee, 1997). Economic factors such as growth rate and/inflation rate can be very important in the short term, but these indicators may change and lose their importance in the long term. Another example is the political stability of the country. This factor may be unimportant at first, but after a crisis, all of the dynamics may change. So, the decision making process should be conducted considering an extensive period of analysis.

The complexity of international plant location decisions makes the possibility of perfectly accurate parameters non-existent. "With all the money and all the time in the world, no expert will ever be able to claim that a parameter, like a ranking for the quality of life in a foreign country, is free of error. The real world is just too dynamic to accurately assess deterministic or for the matter probabilistic parameters for most models" (p. 55, Schniederjans, 1999). Consequently, efficient and effective procedures are required to provide objective data analysis (Benjamin, Chi, Gaber, & Riordan, 1995). The following sections analyze the effectiveness and the efficiency of the different methodologies, which are used to solve plant location problems.

CURRENT METHODOLOGIES

Scaling, Scoring, and Ranking

Scaling, scoring and ranking methods are the easiest and the most applied methods among the plant location selection methods. In scaling and scoring methods, variables or factors are rated numerically whereas in ranking methods, factors are ranked according to the preference of the decision makers.

In scaling methods, decision makers rate the factors on a given scale, one end representing the worst case and the other end representing the best case. Based on this scale, decision makers decide on the importance or the appropriateness of the factors. In scoring methods, a score is given by decision makers. Most of the time, it is on a scale of 100 points but it varies according to the application (Schniederjans, 1999). In scaling and scoring methods, both discrete and continuous variable measures can be applied. In a discrete measurement, decimal numbers are meaningless. For example, if '1' represents a country that offers tax benefits and '0' represents a country that does not offer tax benefits, then '0.3' does not make any sense. In a continuous measurement basis, on the other hand, different answers for a question, such as the quality of labor, can be averaged and a decimal number can represent a meaningful result.

Ranking methods ask decision makers to place criteria into ordered categories. These ranked categories then can be used in decision-making. Highest or lowest rank category may be selected according to the model generated. Usually, a discrete variable measure is used in this method. For example, the importance of the location factors may be asked to rank from '1' to 'n'. In this scale, a decimal number (a continuous measurement basis) will not make any sense (Schniederjans, 1999).

There are different types of data that can be collected for the evaluation and these relate to the 'levels of measurement' of the data. The level of measurement is important since it helps the decision-makers decide how to interpret the data from the variable. In addition, the decision-makers can decide the appropriate statistical analysis

27

according to the levels of measure of the data.[3] There exist four levels of measurement that can be used to identify the limitations of data (Schniederjans, 1999).

1. **Nominal level** involves a count of the frequency of the cases assigned to the various categories. The data can not be ranked, ordered or scaled (Schniederjans, 1999). For example, the number of suppliers available in a foreign country is nominal since they either do exist or do not exist.

2. **Ordinal level** data can be ranked and be put into categories in some order. For example, the quality of education in a foreign country.

3. **Interval (cardinal) level** has equal units of measurement. It permits the same categorization as nominal data and ranking as ordinal data, but adds scaling within each of the ranked categories. Factors examined are placed in two or more groups, which belong to an ordered series, e.g., not important, important, and very important.

4. **Ratio level** is the highest level of measurement[4]. It possesses all of the previous levels' features. In addition, it has the unique feature of an interval category of zero. This enables a meaningful fraction (or ratio) with a ratio variable. For example, the number of suppliers in a country is a ratio. There may be zero suppliers one year ago and there may be twice as many suppliers this year as compared to last year.

All of the levels stated above are applicable for plant location decision making. However, misusing levels of measurement appears as one of the biggest problems in model construction. Data at different levels should not be evaluated in the same process. Specifically, if they are mixed together, it can be an inappropriate comparison (Schniederjans, 1999). After highlighting the importance of data evaluation, the use of data in scaling, scoring and ranking methodologies will be examined next.

---

[3] http://trochim.human.cornell.edu/kb/measlevl.htm

[4] http://www.fao.org/docrep/W3241E/w3241e04.htm#levels of measurement

The sequence in scaling and scoring methods is as follows:

1. The important location factors are selected based on the strategic objectives of the company.

2. Information about the factors is collected for each candidate country.

3. Decision makers rate each factor using an appropriate scale or score.

Once the ratings for each possible location are determined, a total score is calculated by summing up the ratings. The country with the largest total will be the best country in which to locate the plant. If the importance of the factors is not equal, in other words, if one factor is more important than the other, the approach of weighting the importance of the criteria with a *mathematical weighting factor* is used. The larger the weight, the greater the importance of that particular criterion would be. In this case, an expected or weighted total value is calculated by multiplying the mathematical weighting factor by the scales or scores. The weighting factors differ from company to company. The determination of the weighting factor depends on the strategic objectives of the particular company (Schniederjans, 1999).

Scaling and scoring methods have historically been used in making location decisions. In the early 1970s, researchers started to use these methods in plant location decision making (Hoffman & Schniederjans, 1994; Schniederjans, 1999). In ranking method, the location factors are ranked by the decision makers. A total is taken at the end to decide the country. A weighting factor can also be an application here based on the importance of the factors. (Schniederjans, 1999).

Advantages

Scaling, scoring and ranking methods have two considerable advantages. First, they are easy to apply. Second, the decision makers can deal with a large number of data in a simple fashion. The methods permit consideration of an unlimited number of criteria, weighted and/or ordered to fit the needs of the decision makers. The decision

29

makers can include as many location factors as she wants to make the process comprehensive (Schniederjans, 1999) [5].

The ranking method specifically forces an ordinal separation of location factors that may more closely imitate the desired selection decision as opposed to a continuous measure where fractional values can appear as a result and make the decision questionable (Schniederjans, 1999).

Consequently, since the decision makers can easily apply these methods at each level of decision making to evaluate a vast amount of data this method serves very well to the *multi-criteria* and *multilevel* characteristics of the international plant location decisions.

Disadvantages

Although these methods are simple and easy to apply, they have some disadvantages. First of all, decision makers can make errors while scaling/scoring/ranking process, namely sampling errors like estimation in parameters, and their selection. In general, Type I and Type II errors are the concepts that are related to sampling error. Type I error is the case where the best facility is not chosen. A type II error is the case where the less-than-best facility is chosen (Schniederjans, 1999). Objective measures can be more accurately estimated by taking larger samples. Subjective data can be enhanced by asking a large sample of individuals or groups. On the other hand, Schniederjans(1999) suggests that some accuracy may be permitted using sensitivity analysis. "Sensitivity analysis is a set of methodologies that can be used to define boundaries that parameters can be permitted to vary with little or no impact on an existing solution." (p. 54, Schniederjans, 1999)

Another problem is the proportionality of the data. "Proportionality refers to the structuring of measures to reflect their proportioned variation regardless of what type of

---

[5] http://www.rdg.ac.uk/ssc/dfid/booklets/topasd.html#aa12datatypes

scale, score or ranking method is used to depict their value" (p. 54, Schniederjans, 1999). If different levels of measurement are used in the same model, data should be converted to a common basis so that all of them can be analyzed in the same model.

An important drawback of the methodologies is that the scaling/scoring/ranking algorithms do not consider the fact that the criteria may be dependent on each other. For example, decision makers may not be able to rank the importance of labor costs and the inflation rate of a country on the same scale since the increase in the inflation rate may cause an increase in the labor cost. So, the independence of the criteria assumption can cause inconsistency in the results.

Ranking methods, specifically, have a drawback. Results are less informative than scoring; especially if respondents are forced to choose between some nearly equal alternatives and some very different ones.[6]

The most significant disadvantage of these methods is that they disregard the *multi-periodic* characteristic of the international plant location decisions. The selection process is only based on the current information about the factors of the related countries. Uncertainty can be included as a factor; however, the prediction about the other factors still can not be taken into consideration leading to an incomplete analysis for a location.

Analytic Hierarchy Process (AHP)

Analytic Hierarchy Process (AHP) is another decision-making technique for international plant location decisions. AHP was developed by Saaty in 1980 (Saaty, 1988). This is a structured decision-making methodology, which is suitable for complicated situations. It involves decomposing a complex and unstructured problem into a multilevel hierarchy (Yang & Lee, 1997). In this way, several quantitative and qualitative factors can be evaluated in a systematic manner on the basis of multi-criteria

---

[6] http://www.rdg.ac.uk/ssc/dfid/booklets/topasd.html#aa12datatypes

decisions of a competing or conflicting nature (Badri, 1999; Schniederjans & Garvin, 1997) .

AHP methodology requires selecting one or more countries from several candidate countries. In the model, the objective of the organization, the criteria and alternatives are defined and presented in a hierarchic form.   An example of a hierarchy is represented in Figure 6.

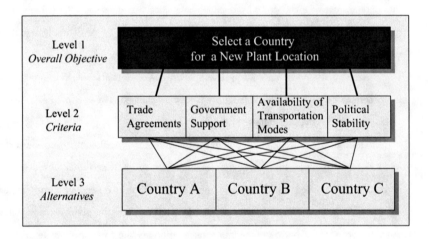

Figure 6 A hierarchy for an international plant location decision

AHP methodology involves five steps in solving a decision problem:

1. <u>Problem Decomposition:</u> The problem should be decomposed into the different levels to form the hierarchy of interrelated decision elements (Saaty, 1994; Zahedi, 1986). Each element should further be decomposed into sub-elements until the lowest level of the hierarchy (Saaty, 1994). Basically, the overall objective, criteria and decision alternatives of the problem should be represented in the graphical representation(Badri, 1999).(See Figure 6)

2. <u>Comparative Analysis:</u> In this step, the relative importance of each criterion in terms of its contribution to the achievement of the overall objective should be

32

determined (Badri, 1999). So, the decision makers should specify a priority or a preference for each alternative via pairwise comparison (Saaty, 1994; Zahedi, 1986) Decision makers provides numerical values for the priority of each element using a rating scale (Saaty, 1994).

3. Synthesis of Priorities: There are two methods to synthesize the priorities. The first one is the AHP approximation method. In this method, weightings of the factors are mathematically converted into a final set of rankings. The greater the weight, the greater the preference for the specific country (alternative) (Badri, 1999; Schniederjans, 1999). The second method to estimate the relative weights of decision elements is the eigenvalue method (Zahedi, 1986). The weights of elements at each level are computed using eigenvector or least square analysis. This process continues for each level of the hierarchy until a final decision is reached (Saaty, 1994) .

4. Determine Consistency: Since the AHP process depends on judgmental decision making, the consistency of these judgments is critical for the dependability and the accuracy) of the AHP method in decision making. The evaluation of the decision makers' judgmental consistency is realized by computing a consistency ratio (CR) statistics (Schniederjans, 1999)

5. Aggregation: As a last step, the relative weights of decision elements should be aggregated to arrive at a set of ratings for the alternative countries (Schniederjans, 1999; Zahedi, 1986).

Yurimoto and Masui (1995) applied the AHP method to model the selection process of a location for Japanese affiliates in the EU. In their research, they developed a hierarchy for location factors and assigned evaluation indices for each location factors of the last level (Figure 7).

33

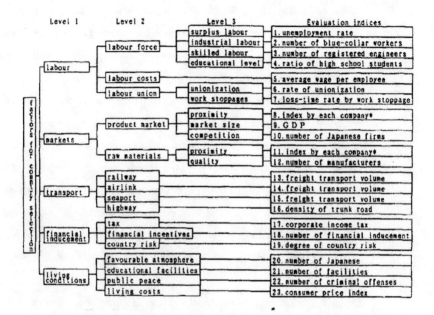

Figure 7 A Hierarchical structure of location factors for a company selection (Yurimoto & Masui, 1995)

First, data related to the location factors and evaluation indices for each country were collected. Then, weightings were assigned according to a scale of 1 to 10. The preference weight of the decision makers were calculated according to the AHP procedure and the optimal location that had the highest weight for related factors was reached. As a result of their research, the countries where Japanese companies actually established affiliates appeared in the upper rank in the final ranking.

Yang and Lee (1997) used the AHP methodology only in determining goal priorities and objective function weights in a goal programming formulation, to examine the weighting vector within the reference framework. They searched reference direction in a visual interactive system, and identified objective coefficient and parameter values in multiple objective problems.

34

Considering these two applications of the AHP methodology, it can be concluded that there exist advantages and disadvantages of using this method as a decision making tool.

Advantages

The advantages of the AHP methodology, basically, stem from two fundamentals of the approach: the hierarchical structure and the pairwise comparison.

Yang and Lee (1997) stated that organizing a complex problem using a hierarchy has the following advantages:

1. It provides a general outlook of the complex relationships in the problem.

2. It helps decision-makers judge the issues in each level in terms of order of magnitude. So, homogeneity in comparisons is preserved.

3. It provides a framework for seeking input about the factors and sub factors within the hierarchy from different levels of managers in the organization.

4. A hierarchical structure can easily be incorporated into an interactive solution, which allows active participation of the managers involved in the solution process.

Most of the time, the direct assignment of weights to the factors is too abstract for the decision makers and results in inaccuracies. The AHP approach compares only two alternatives at a time (Badri, 1999). These pairwise comparisons give the decision makers a basis on which to express a level of preference by comparing two alternatives(Badri, 1999; Zahedi, 1986) This characteristic of the AHP, on one hand, allows decision makers to express his or her preferential expert judgment in the decision making process (Badri, 1999). Whereas, on the other hand, the decision makers' subjective judgments can be quantified by assigning corresponding numerical values based on the relative importance of factors under consideration(Yang & Lee, 1997).

Consequently, AHP methodology fits the two main characteristics, the *multi-level* and *multi-criteria* nature, of the international plant location decisions very well. Multi-levelness can be expressed by the hierarchic form in the methodology. The multi-criteria characteristic of the decision (several candidate countries (alternatives) with a large number of qualitative and quantitative factors) can easily be dealt with the AHP since its methodology requires selecting one or more countries from several candidate countries.

Disadvantages

The disadvantages of the AHP method mostly stem from the decision makers. Zahedi (1986) stated that the decision makers might be inconsistent in expressing his/her preferences during pairwise comparison. Yang & Lee (1997) supported this disadvantage and added that besides inconsistency, the priority weights could vary from decision makers to decision makers and achieving consensus might be difficult. For the same disadvantage, Schniederjans and Garvin (1997) argued that an appropriate level of consistency is necessary to achieve meaningful results although perfect consistency is not achievable. To overcome this drawback, a consistency index is calculated to determine the accuracy of the results.

Another drawback is the limitation in the number of elements to compare. Saaty (1988) suggested that the number of elements at each level should be limited to a maximum of nine to provide consistent result, since each level entails pairwise comparisons of its elements. In addition, possible constraints are not directly considered in the selection process because of the nature of the model. (Badri, 1999; Schniederjans & Garvin, 1997).

An important disadvantage, like scaling/scoring/ranking methods, is that AHP disregards the multi-period characteristic of the international plant location analysis. The selection process only considers the current situation. Uncertainty can be incorporated in the model as a criterion, however, it is hard to consider the effect of this addition on the other criteria. For example, a country with high uncertainty may have an economic crisis, and labor costs may increase due to the crisis. In this case, the decision makers can evaluate the uncertainty in the country, but they may not reflect this uncertainty to their comparisons for other criteria. So, this may be a serious deficiency in the AHP model depending on the preferences of the decision makers.

Mathematical Programming

Mathematical programming is structuring a model in mathematical notation. The decision makers seek an optimal solution that satisfies a set of constraints (i.e. a capacity limitation or a budgetary limitation) (Schniederjans, 1999).

Different types of mathematical models are used in plant location decisions. The most common ones are:

- Linear Programming (LP)
- Integer Programming (IP)
- Goal Programming (GP)

A linear programming model is an optimization model which attempts to maximize/minimize a linear function of the decision variables while satisfying a set of constraints. An integer programming model is a form of linear programming model in which some or all of the variables are required to be nonnegative integers (Winston, 1994). In goal programming, the nature of the objective function is different. LP and IP are uni-objective models. In other words, they only have one objective to maximize/minimize. In many situations, however, the action chosen depends on how each possible objective affects more than one attribute or variable. For example, the selection of a plant location should always satisfy multiple objectives by considering both the quantitative and the qualitative factors (Chuang, 2001). Goal programming is designed to deal with these multiple objectives. These objectives are stated as

37

constraints in the model and a combined objective function is created in order to reach the target values (Schniederjans, 1999).

Extensive research has been conducted about plant location problems in the management science and operations management literature. In this literature, plant location problems can be classified into three areas as follows (Lim & Kim, 1999):

- Static (single period) plant location problems
- Dynamic (multiperiod) uncapacitated plant location problems
- Dynamic capacitated plant location problems

Based on the classification above, plant location problems have two dimensions: time and space. Time is the first dimension of the plant location problems. In the literature surveyed, models are based either on a single period or multiple periods. In a single period (static) model, all decisions are made at a single point in time. Multi-period (dynamic) models arise when the decision maker makes decisions at more than one point in time. Dynamic programming is used to solve the multi-period problems. The solving mechanism of dynamic programming is working backward from the end of a problem toward the beginning, thus breaking up a large, unwieldy problem into a series of smaller, more tractable problems (Winston, 1994).

Most of the models developed in the literature are static, deterministic models. In these models, all inputs (demands, distances, transportation times, etc.) are considered as known quantities and outputs are taken as one-time decision values (Owen & Daskin, 1998). However, plant location decisions are frequently long-term decisions since they require large capital investments. Hence, a multi-period approach is more appropriate to reach a realistic solution. Besides, there may be considerable uncertainty in the environment that may affect the values of the selected parameters in the location decision (Current, Ratick, & ReVelle, 1997). Unfortunately, the deterministic models cannot represent the uncertainty in the real world. So, plant location problems should include either stochastic or dynamic problem characteristics because the dynamic models

38

incorporate time and the stochastic models incorporate uncertainty (Current et al., 1997; Owen & Daskin, 1998). Current et al. (1997) stated that since the pioneering work of (Manne, 1961, 1967) and (Ballou, 1968), there has been a significant interest in dynamic location modeling. In their article they also listed articles that explicitly addressed dynamic location problems (Current et al., 1997).

On the second dimension of the plant location problems, extensive modeling work has been done. However, there exists very little modeling research on global facility location problems (Canel & Das, 2002). More research on this subject is needed which expands the mathematical models to incorporate location factors, such as exchange rates, political stability, government incentives, etc.

Several different deterministic models have been formulated to solve plant location problems (Brimberg & ReVelle, 1999, 2000; Canel & Das, 2002; Canel & Khumawala, 1997; Current et al., 1997; Houshyar & White, 1997; Lim & Kim, 1999; Schmidt & Wilhelm, 2000; Tombak, 1995). And detailed surveys of plant location research have been mentioned in several articles. Tombak (1995) cited a survey of the non-competitive models in the literature. Canel and Das (2002) mentioned that vast literature exists about quantitative modeling. Houshyar and White (1997) noted that in the last three decades a variety of models have been developed to solve facility location problems and added that most of the techniques have been reviewed by many researchers. In addition to this source, Owen and Daskin (1998) cited many published review articles or texts in their research.

Advantages

Mathematical programming models reach an optimal solution in the end if the problem is formulated correctly and the appropriate inputs are selected. Linear programming models can reach an optimal solution easily. IPs are generally harder to solve than LPs (Winston, 1994), unless the problem is very small or has special

39

characteristics despite potentially long computation times. Finding the global optimum rather than reaching a local optimum or a near-optimum solution is the strongest characteristic of these methods.

Another important advantage is that the number of criteria or location factors that can be used is virtually unlimited in mathematical programming models (Schniederjans, 1999). This advantage serves well to the needs of the multi-criteria characteristic of international plant location decisions.

Models can be developed both in a static and a dynamic fashion with mathematical programming. However, in international plant location selections, dynamic programming is necessary because of the multi-period characteristic of the decisions. They provide a better overall appraisal of the essential requirements for international plant location decisions.

Disadvantages

Mathematical programming models require some assumptions to be met in order to accurately arrive at an optimal solution (Schniederjans, 1999). First of all, all parameters must be known with certainty. Otherwise, the model will not provide the optimal solution. This requirement causes disadvantages since it is not always possible to get the exact data for each parameter. The decision makers are then forced to assume some conditions to meet the desired objective. These assumptions, which are different than the assumptions for other methodologies like simulation, make the result unrealistic for real world applications. As an example, Plastria (2001) stated that a large part of location theory in operational research has adopted the modeling assumption of a spatial monopoly: the company offers a unique product or service and is the single player in the part of the market that is considered (Plastria, 2001). However, in practice, there is more than one product and more than one player in the market for a company. Another example is given by Revelle and Laporte (1996). They stated that the cost of transportation has an ambiguous origin in the models. It could have been calculated by a linearty assumption or a general concave function or a fixed-charge cost function (ReVelle & Laporte, 1996). Although researchers are aware of the unrealistic approach of making many assumptions to model the problem, there is no other way to run the model and to reach an optimal solution without making assumptions. So, the advantages of incorporating unlimited amount of factors and reaching an optimal solution in the end are questionable under these circumstances.

The accuracy of the model completely depends on the selection of the parameters since each unit of the decision variable contributes a constant unit (selected parameter) to the objective function and in the constraint (Schniederjans, 1999). If an incorrect coefficient(s) is used, the contribution of that variable to the objective function or to the constraints will be inaccurate. Hence, determination of the coefficients is critical and may appear as a disadvantage for some cases.

Based on the disadvantages stated above, producing an optimal solution to the plant location problem is quite difficult or impossible even though mathematical programming permits various variables to be theoretically included in the model. Moreover, based on the characteristics of the plant location problems, the objective function might not contain certain properties (differentiable, continuous, etc.) and even it might not be an actual function.

For accuracy, one should make sure that a sensitivity analysis of the parameters that are critical should be accomplished. Another limitation is that, in the traditional type of sensitivity analysis for analyzing the effect of the change in the factors, only a single change can be accomplished at a time. Multiple changes can be examined by using the model as a simulation tool. The change can be observed by making a parameter change in the model and resolving the problem to see the simulated effect of the change in the new solution (Hoffman & Schniederjans, 1994). For some LPs it might not be a problem, but for IPs, it may cause a problem because of the solution time.

41

Heuristic Algorithms

A heuristic is a formulation serving as a guide in the solution of a problem. There are many heuristic algorithms. Tabu search algorithms, genetic algorithms (GAs) and neural networks (NNs) will be the algorithms used as the subject of this chapter. These heuristic methods are generally called extended neighborhood search (ENS) algorithms (Schniederjans, 1999).

Basically, heuristic algorithms try to find the optimal solution, in a defined set, by comparing each solution with the previous one. Based on the comparison, the objective function improves until some criterion such as time limit, is met. For example, in Figure

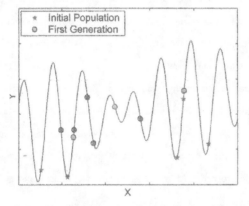

8, the function shows the feasible solutions from a genetic algorithm (GA) problem. In this figure, the initial population (solutions) is enhanced after an iteration of the heuristic algorithm and the first generation is formed (a better set of solutions).

Figure 8 An iteration in a heuristic algorithm (Joines, 2002)

These iterations continue to attempt to reach a better solution at each trial. One example might be deciding the right countries according to a profit maximization objective function. Countries can be added/ removed by comparing the profit at each iteration. If the profit enhances, the country is added to the solution set. If the profit decreases, then it won't be added to the set. The attractive characteristic of these algorithms is that they can randomly search different places in a huge population of possible solutions.

This extensive search capability improves the chance of reaching the global optimal solution. Since the search is conducted nearby or in neighborhood values, these algorithms are called extended neighborhood search (ENS) algorithms.

Tabu search algorithms and genetic algorithms (GAs) are ENS algorithms. They conduct search and reach solution as stated above. One unique feature of GAs is the possibility of mutations and crossovers. Genetic algorithm is based on the evolution theory. GAs work with a population of parents and their children. Each of these represents a possible solution to the problem. Children's genes are inherited from their parents or combined in an unexpected way by mutations and crossovers to provide diversification. Unlike Tabu search algorithms, GAs have the ability to avoid a singular path in solving a problem with the aid of this feature. The population can evolve towards better solutions with the aid of randomized processes of selection, crossover and mutation (Kratice, Tosic, Filipovic, & Ljubic, 2001).

Neural Networks, on the other hand, mimic brain function (Bauer, 1994). They check alternatives as they progress through the network of possible solutions. In this way, they learn and explore directions where better solutions might be obtained. Thus, the NN algorithms improve through usage. "Plant location problem solving might become more and more efficient regardless of different location factors that are used in each study"(Schniederjans, 1999).

In the literature, the affinity to heuristic algorithms has improved as the need to serve the real world has increased.[7] Canel and Khumawala (2001) developed and tested heuristic approaches for solving the uncapacitated multi-period international facility location problem. Badri (1999) and Chuang (2001) have stated in their research that (Klincewicz, 1985) developed an efficient heuristic for a complex single-period facility location; (Holmberg, Ronnqvist, & Yuan, 1999) and (Ronnqvist, 1999) proposed a primal heuristic for a single source-capacitated facility location problems. Benjamin et al.

---

[7] The reason will be discussed in the *Advantages* section of this chapter.

(1995) developed two Artificial NN (ANN) models to classify the 48 states in the continental USA based on their suitability for locating manufacturing facilities. Verter and Dasci (2002) modeled the plant location problem as a mixed integer nonlinear program and suggested heuristic and exact solution methods that iteratively solve a series of mixed integer linear program. The computational results were quite satisfactory (Verter & Dasci, 2002). Nevertheless, differentiating factors of international plant location (e.g. exchange rate and price uncertainties, tariffs and quotes) were not included in the model.

Advantages

The main advantage of the ENS algorithms is the effective processing capability of the algorithms. They can find near optimal solutions in very large sets of data, where other algorithmic approaches (like integer programming) might not be able to solve the problem (Schniederjans, 1999).

These algorithms are not based on some strong assumptions like linear programming. Among other possibilities, one can incorporate non-linear constraints in the model. This flexibility is another major advantage for this methodology.

Universally, there is not any clear conclusion that Tabu search is better than GAs or vice versa. However, Tabu search algorithms permit the solution to move toward an inferior solution temporarily to achieve a more global solution in the final decision (Schniederjans, 1999). According to Schniederjans (1999), GAs are even more successful than Tabu search algorithm since they can generate a diversification and increase the chance to reach a global optimum by crossovers and mutation. Another advantage of GAs is their ability to start working with a randomly constructed population of initial guesses to the problem solution. Therefore, it is possible to start up a GA procedure with only little knowledge (Bauer, 1994). They are fast and flexible and hence they are very effective for analyzing possible international plant locations.

NNs are ideal for the problems where the data are highly variable or uncertain. They can locate a variety of decision paths that meet a set of criteria or constraints, which the decision maker wants to accomplish (Schniederjans, 1999). As a result, the advantages of heuristic algorithms meet the needs of international plant location decisions. Multi-criteria, multi-level and multi-periodical characteristics of international plant location decisions are fulfilled with the aid of the capabilities of the algorithms.

Disadvantages

Tabu search algorithms incorporate a disadvantage because of their logic. There exists a sequential process in the algorithm, which does not let the decision maker try as many different combinations as GAs to reach a global optimum (near-optimum). The subsequent selection limits the current decision. Opportunities which may exist in the neighborhood of payoff values may not be taken into consideration (Schniederjans, 1999).

In the case of GAs, the first disadvantage is their poor performance in small data sets. Schniederjans (1999) stated that GAs would be ideal when large amount of data needs to be analyzed. Kratice et al.'s (2001) research has proved this and they proposed a genetic algorithm to solve a simple plant location problem (SPLP). They found that the algorithm was effective to solve SPLP which involved more than 1000 facility sites and customers (Kratice et al., 2001). The second disadvantage for genetic algorithms is that problems must be translated into a suitable form for GAs and this translation can be difficult for some cases (Bauer, 1994).

Overall, the heuristic algorithms seem to fit the requirements of international plant location decisions, however, one should not forget that the result is not always the optimal solution. Most of the time, based on the population and the run time, near-optimal solutions can be reached at the end. However, for practical use, these results may still serve the needs of the real world.

45

Simulation

Simulation is a technique to mimic the operations of various kinds of real world facilities or processes, usually on a computer with appropriate software (Kelton, Sadowski, & Sadowski, 2002; Law & Kelton, 2000). When the relationships that compose the model are not simple enough to use mathematical methods (such as algebra, calculus and probability theory), simulation is used to evaluate the models.

Determining the objective of a simulation is a starting point for the process. This is followed by a set of steps to develop the simulation model, and eventually the model is run to generate some results (Schniederjans, 1999). The steps of the simulation process are as follows:

1. Definition of the problem

2. Formulation of the model

3. Validation of the model

4. Generation of the results after simulation runs

5. Analysis of the results

6. Decision Making based on the analysis

An example of the formulation step is depicted in Figure 9.

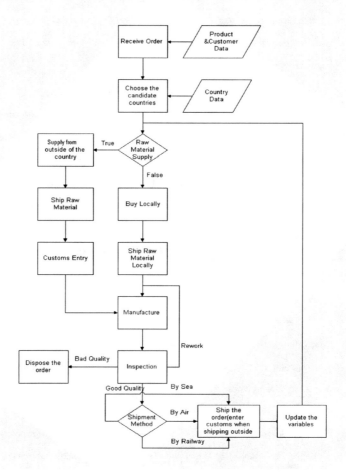

Figure 9 Simulation model

There are a few studies that have used simulation models for international plant location selection in the literature. One comprehensive study has been conducted by Chakravarty (1999). He has developed a simulation model that incorporated the role of country-specific variables (e.g. economic growth, labor and material cost, tax and tariff

47

rates) into the model in order to determine the pattern of long-term investments in manufacturing plants (Chakravarty, 1999). The factors are calculated using a mathematical model; however, not all of the important location factors were included in the model.

Advantages

Simulation models are often viewed as a default methodology in management science because they can deal with unlimited variables and parameters (Schniederjans, 1999). They can incorporate uncertainty by considering a required change during a required period of time. With these features, simulation fits as an appropriate model for international plant location decisions. Considering the main characteristics of these decisions, simulation appears to be good match.

Disadvantages

Simulation is not an optimization tool. It can mimic the problem realistically. Some results can be generated based on the variables and parameters entered, however, these results might not be the optimal results. To avoid this disadvantage, a sensitivity analysis can be applied to reach an optimal result. In addition, some simulation programs include an optimization toolbox. At the end of the run, this optimization software can be run with required changes in the selected parameters and the optimum result can be obtained accordingly.

Simulation requires the selection of different types of probability distributions to model the behavior of the random variables. Manufacturing time, order creation time, transportation time are some examples which need a probability distribution. However, it is not always easy to determine the correct type of the distribution, which represents real world applications. Using an inaccurate distribution may lead to incorrect analysis in the end.

Like heuristic algorithms, exact information cannot be obtained by simulation. However, most real world systems are too complex to be evaluated by analytical methods. Law and Kelton (2000) stated that these models must be studied by means of simulation.

CONCLUSION

Different methodologies offering different decision making techniques are analyzed for plant location selection. Models, mainly based on the decision maker's preferences (Scaling, scoring, ranking, AHP), traditional mathematical programming models, latest solution methodologies (Heuristic algorithms and simulation) are examined. After a detailed analysis for each methodology, the advantages and disadvantages of the methodologies for international plant location are summarized in Table 2 considering the important factors for international plant location decisions.

Table 2 Advantages and disadvantages of the methodologies

	Model Construction	Model Usage	Solution Generation
Scaling/ Scoring/ Ranking (SSR)	• Easy to develop • Theoretically, they can handle large amount of location factors • Sampling errors • Proportionality of data • Unable to incorporate uncertainty in the environment • Single period is considered during construction	• Easy to apply • In practice, if large amount of location factors are considered, it is not that easy to give a consistent comparison	• Solution is based on the preferences of the decision-makers • It can not be defined as an optimum solution since some important aspects (such as uncertainty in the environment) is ignored during the analysis
AHP	• Hierarchical form provides homogeneity in comparisons (A) • The number of elements to compare should be limited to a maximum of nine at each level for consistency	• Pairwise comparison provides an easier comparison than direct assignment of weights to the factors	• Consistency of the results is questionable (like in SSR) • The solution can not be defined as an optimum solution (like in SSR)

49

Table 2 (con't)			
Mathematical Programming	• Theoretically, a large amount of location factors can be handled • Unrealistic assumptions are made • Model construction is critical since the accuracy of the model completely depends on the selection of the parameters • It is not easy to construct a realistic algorithm • Uncertainty may be involved in stochastic and dynamic models	• Impractical sensitivity analysis especially for IPs (because of the solution time) • Technologic developments eased the usage of mathematical programming algorithms	• The solution is an exact (optimal solution) • Although the factors that can be incorporated in the algorithm are theoretically unlimited, complex algorithms is hard to solve. • IPs are generally harder to solve than LPs
Heuristic Algorithms	• Uncertainty can be involved • Extensive period analysis can be constructed easily • Strong assumptions like in LPs are not needed. • GAs can start with only little knowledge • GAs require the translation of the problem into a suitable form.	• They are fast and easy to apply	• Poor performance in small data sets. • A near optimal solution can be reached most of the time • High chance to reach the global optimum solution
Simulation	• Unlimited criteria can be handled in the algorithm • Uncertainty can be incorporated in the algorithm • Appropriate probability distributions can not be found to model the behavior of the random variables		• Optimal solution might not be obtained since simulation is not an optimization tool

Scaling, scoring, ranking and AHP methods are simple and effective methods that serve both the multilevel and multi-criteria characteristics of international plant location decisions. However, only current conditions can be evaluated with these methods.

Uncertainty in the environment is hard to model for these methodologies. In AHP, uncertainty can be incorporated in the model as a criterion; however, it is hard to consider the effect of this addition on the other criteria. Besides, solutions will solely be based on the preferences of the decision makers since the structure of the decisions; scaling, scoring, ranking and pairwise comparisons are asked to decision makers to be performed. AHP reduces inconsistency with the pairwise comparison but still; the required consistency cannot be reached at the end. Decision makers who want an easy method to consider multiple criteria for each level of the analysis should use these methods, being aware of their limitations.

Mathematical modeling techniques offer an exact solution with the ability to incorporate unlimited number of factors into the model. However, each parameter should be known correctly. Since this situation is impossible for every parameter, some assumptions have to be made to be able to calculate the exact figures. These assumptions might not be realistic when real world applications are concerned. However, this situation may be improved by the recently commenced research to include the stochastic approach and multi- periodical analysis in their models for plant location decisions. Given these facts, mathematical models generate optimum solution with unrealistic assumptions and sometimes with impractical models. Decision makers who accept these limitations and seek an accurate solution should use mathematical models for international plant location decisions. In addition these models could be used to determine the input structure for the heuristic or simulation models.

In the literature, the affinity to heuristic algorithms and simulation methodologies has improved as the need to serve the real world has increased. Heuristics are fast and flexible algorithms, which can consider all of the characteristics of international plant location decisions. They can incorporate unlimited number of factors and solve the algorithm fast with the aid of computers. However, an optimum solution might not be reached for each trial. Most of the time, based on the population and the run time,

51

results would be near-optimal. However, for practical use, these results may still serve the needs of the real world. Decision makers who seek a realistic but a near optimal solution that considers most of the practical factors and conditions should choose heuristic algorithms for international plant location decisions.

Simulation models mimic the real world. Decision makers model the circumstances and factors that they want and run the simulation to obtain results. Unfortunately, it is not always easy to find the appropriate probability function to model the behavior of the random variables. Besides, results only represent the modeled conditions. They are not optimum results in that sense. A sensitivity analysis should be implemented by changing the desired variables and by examining the change in the overall results, or an optimization toolbox should be used at the end of the simulation to reach an optimal solution. This method is very flexible and lets user decide whatever s/he wants. Decision makers who want to model the current conditions in their company and in their environment and want to analyze the future in specific circumstances should use simulation for international plant location decisions. An optimization tool is necessary at the end for an optimal solution. The selected methodologies according to the decision makers' requirements are summarized in Figure 10.

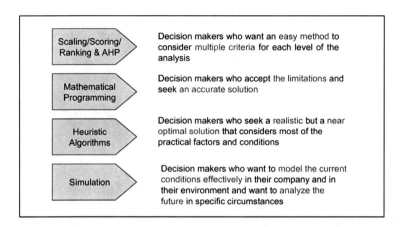

Figure 10 A summary of the characteristics of the selected methodologies

When the suitability of the selected methodologies is evaluated according to the characteristics of international plant location decisions, only scaling/scoring/ranking and AHP methodologies seem to be incompatible in serving to the multi-periodic needs of international plant location decisions. Other methodologies are appropriate for all of the defined characteristics. However, critical concerns under these characteristics should also be analyzed to reach an accurate decision for which methodology to choose. These concerns are stated below:

1. If the method is
   - easy to develop
   - easy to apply
   - fast
   - flexible
   - dynamic
   - realistic

2. If the method can incorporate uncertainty

3. If the method can deal with unlimited number of criteria

4. If the solution is an optimal solution.

The comparison of the methodologies is presented in Figure 11.

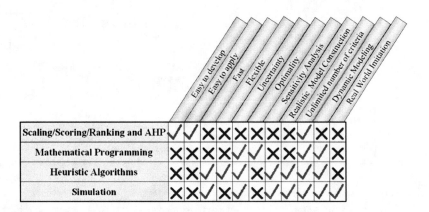

Figure 11 Comparison of the current methodologies in terms of the critical factors for international plant location decisions

Textile and apparel companies, first, have to choose the most important factors according to their organizational culture and corporate strategy. Based on the number of factors, the product types that are planning to be produced and the expected strategic gain of the company, the appropriate methodology should be determined. The comparison chart in Figure 11 can provide a structure for the analysis.

In today's environment, uncertainty or risk incorporation is the most critical concern for textile and apparel industries. With the elimination of tariffs and quotas in 2005, and several trade agreements such as NAFTA and CBI, textile and apparel companies are forced to do business in such a volatile environment. In this respect, scaling/scoring/ ranking methods and AHP are easy to develop and use but they are incompetent in reflecting a good snapshot for the future, especially, when uncertainty and risk in the environment are concerned. For textile and apparel industries, especially for textile industry, a more accurate prediction of the future is critical since the level of investment is really high. Then, the models that can incorporate uncertainty, like mathematical programming, heuristic algorithms and simulation appear as the appropriate methodologies. In addition, developing realistic models using mathematical programming is limited because of the strict assumptions such as linearity. If companies may release the need for an accurate (exact) solution, heuristics and simulation would remain as the most appropriate methods for textile and apparel industry.

Overall, all of the methodologies, explained in this paper, have advantages and disadvantages when international plant location decisions are concerned. Decision makers should decide the right solution for the needs of their company and the current market dynamics. There is always a possibility to use these decisions in a combined fashion. Limitations might be diminished by using a combined method for international plant location selection. Future research may analyze the combinations of these different methodologies to reach a better solution.

REFERENCES

Badri, M. A. (1999). Combining the Analytic Hierarchy Process and Goal Programming for Global Facility Location-Allocation Problem. International Journal of Production Economics, 62, 237-248.

Ballou, R. H. (1968). Dynamic Warehouse Location Analysis. Journal of Marketing Research, 7, 271-276.

Bauer, R. J., Jr. (1994). Genetic Algorithms and Investment Strategies. New York: John Wiley & Sons, Inc.

Benjamin, C. O., Chi, S., Gaber, T., & Riordan, C. A. (1995). Comparing BP and ART II Neural Network Classifiers for Facility Location. Computers and Industrial Engineering, 28(1), 43-50.

Brimberg, J., & ReVelle, C. (1999). A multi-facility location model with partial satisfaction of demand. Studies in Locational Analysis, 13, 91-101.

Brimberg, J., & ReVelle, C. (2000). The maximum return-on-investment plant location. Journal of the Operational Research Society, 51, 729-735.

Canel, C., & Das, S., R. (2002). Modeling Global Facility Location Decisions:Integrating Marketing and Manufacturing Decisions. Industrial Management & Data Systems, 102(2), 110-118.

Canel, C., & Khumawala, B. M. (1997). Multi-period international facilities location:an algorithm and application. International Journal of Production Research, 35(7), 1891-1910.

Chakravarty, A. K. (1999). Profit margin, process improvement and capacity decisions in global manufacturing. International Journal of Production Research, 37(18), 4235-4257.

Chuang, P. T. (2001). Combining the Analytical Hierarchy Process and Quality Function Deployment for a Location Decision from a Requirement Perspective. The International Journal of Advanced Manufacturing Technology, 18, 842-849.

Current, J., Ratick, S., & ReVelle, C. (1997). Dynamic Facility Location When the Total Number of Facilities is Uncertain: A Decision Analysis Approach. European Journal of Operational Research, 110, 597-609.

Hoffman, J. J., & Schniederjans, M. J. (1994). A Two-stage Model for Structuring Global Facility Site Selection Decisions. International Journal of Operations & Production Management, 14(4), 79-96.

Holmberg, K., Ronnqvist, M., & Yuan, D. (1999). An Exact Algorithm for the Capacitated Facility Location Problems with Single Sourcing. European Journal of Operational Research, 113(3), 544-559.

Houshyar, A., & White, B. (1997). Comparison of Solution Procedures to the Facility Location Problem. Computers and Industrial Engineering, 32(1), 77-87.

Joines, J. A. (2002). TE589D Evolutionary Optimization Class Notes.

Kelton, W. D., Sadowski, R. P., & Sadowski, D. A. (2002). Simulation with Arena (Second edition ed.): Mc Graw Hill.

Klincewicz, J. G. (1985). A large-scale Distribution and Location Model. AT&T Technical Journal, 64, 1705-1730.

Kratice, J., Tosic, D., Filipovic, V., & Ljubic, I. (2001). Solving the simple plant location problem by genetic algorithm. RAIRO Operations Research, 35, 127-142.

Law, A. M., & Kelton, W. D. (2000). Simulation Modeling and Analysis (Third Edition ed.): Mc Graw Hill.

Lim, S. K., & Kim, Y. D. (1999). An Integrated Approach to Dynamic Plant Loation and Capacity Planning. Journal of the Operational Research Society, 50, 1205-1216.

Manne, A. S. (1961). Capacity Extension and Probabilistic Growth. Econometrica, 29, 632649.

Manne, A. S. (1967). Investments for Capacity Expansion: Size, Location, and Time Phasing. Cambridge, MA: MIT Press.

McDonald, A. L. (1986). Of Floating Factories and Mating Dinosaurs. Harvard Business Review, 64(6), 82-86.

Owen, S. H., & Daskin, M. S. (1998). Strategic Facility Location: A Review. European Journal of Operational Research, 111, 423-447.

Plastria, F. (2001). Static Competitive Facility Location: An Overview of optimization Approaches. European Journal of Operational Research, 129, 461-470.

ReVelle, C., & Laporte, G. (1996). The Plant Location Problem: New Models and Research Prospects. OR Chronicle, 44(6), 864-874.

Ronnqvist, M. (1999). A repeated Matching Heuristic for the Single Source Capacitated Facility Location Problem. European Journal of Operational Research, 116(1), 51-68.

Saaty, T. L. (1988). Multicriteria Decision Making: The Analytic Hierarchy Process. United States.

Saaty, T. L. (1994). Highlights and Critical Points in the Theory and Application of the Analytic Hierarchy Process. European Journal of Operational Research, 74, 426-447.

Schmidt, G., & Wilhelm, W. E. (2000). Strategic, tactical and operational decisions in multi-national logistics networks: a review and discussion of modeling issues. International Journal of Production Research, 38(7), 1501-1523.

Schniederjans, M. J. (1999). International Facility Acquisition and Location Analysis. London: Quorum Books.

Schniederjans, M. J., & Garvin, T. (1997). Using Analytic Hierarchy Process and Multi-objective Programming for the Selection of Cost Drivers in Activity-based Costing. European Journal of Operational Research, 100, 72-80.

Tombak, M. M. (1995). Multinational Plant Location as a Game of Timing. European Journal of Operational Research, 86, 434-451.

Verter, V., & Dasci, A. (2002). The plant location and flexible technology acquisition problem. European Journal of Operational Research, 136, 366-382.

Yang, J., & Lee, H. (1997). An AHP Decision Model for Facility Location Selection. Facilities, 15(9/10 (September/October)), 241-254.

Yurimoto, S., & Masui, T. (1995). Design of a decision support system for overseas plant location in the EC. International Journal of Production Economics, 41, 411-418.

Zahedi, F. (1986). The Analytic Hierarchy Process- A Survey of the Method and its Applications. Interfaces, 16(4(July-August)), 96-108.

PART III: A NEW LIST OF LOCATION FACTORS FOR INTERNATIONAL INVESTMENTS

INTRODUCTION

Investment decisions first caught the attention of researchers in the early 1900s. Starting from 1909 with the location theorist, Alfred Weber, researchers have examined the problem of investing in an appropriate location for companies from different industries.

The investigation started in theory at first. Many location theorists either examined the problem from "different" points of views or enhanced earlier theories. In 1970s, empirical studies started with researchers using different lists of location factors and analyzing the decision-making behaviors of companies using these lists. They considered the list of factors affecting location decisions as relatively constant in their research (Notes on Facility Location, 1989), however, they argued that the importance or weighting of the factors could vary by industry type, sector type, parent company location, etc.

This paper examines the research of the theorists, and the factors that they considered are aggregated in a table to clearly present the important factors for that period of time. Empirical studies are analyzed and the factors in these studies are also aggregated in accordance with the important periods in history. After analyzing both the theoretical and the empirical studies, a "comprehensive location factors list" was developed for investment decisions according to the current environment's needs. A categorization of the factors was performed based on the main important groups: cost, availability, accessibility, quality, risk/uncertainty, easy of operations and quality of life. This list provides the important location factors for companies to consider under meaningful categories, to ease their search for the most appropriate location to invest. By having this composite list, the efforts to find a centralized resource can be reduced.

LITERATURE REVIEW

"By **location factor** we mean an advantage which is gained when an economic activity takes place at a particular point or at several such points rather than elsewhere" (Weber, 1929). Weber continued his argument by stating that an advantage was a saving of cost of any kind. Today, the definition of advantage has changed drastically. Many other evaluation criteria have evolved other than cost, like quality, lead-time, etc. Thus, there is an evolution of plant location factors with history and this is demonstrated in this literature review.

First, historical snapshot is given in Figure 12. This is included to depict the differences in location factors for various time periods. In the figure, the different paradigms that were dominant at different times are shown.

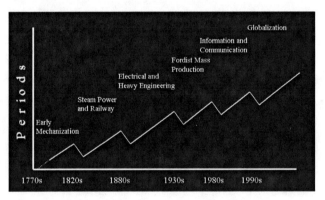

Figure 12 Important periods in history (Adapted from Kondratieff Long Waves (Hayter, 1997))

The evolution of manufacturing began with mechanization and excelled with the invention of steam power. Railway construction enabled transportation of goods to and from different places, and stimulated the possibility of investing and manufacturing in new locations. With the aid of engineering, manufacturing of different goods was

61

expedited and the Fordist mass production paradigm defined flow processes and assembly lines and the 'economies of scale' concept gained importance. Then, with the aid of computers, communication and information sharing became critical and this evolved to the Internet. Today, the world is a "global village". Manufacturing, or investments options are spread to anywhere in the world. Boundaries between countries are diminishing day by day. Companies, now, are trying to gain an advantage to be able to stay competitive in this new pool of competitors.

As indicated above, location factors examined theoretically and then researchers expanded and modified these factors by empirical studies. The evolution of these studies is examined in the following sections.

Location Theory

Several theories have been developed for plant location starting with Alfred Weber (1909), the German economist who published *Uber den Standort der Industrien*. Weber limited his theory to manufacturing, and specifically the location problems of industrial firms (Tong, 1979). His theory is considered to be the first attempt to construct a general theory of the location of all economic activity (Isard, 1956). Weber made assumptions to eliminate many of the complexities of the real world. In Weber's theory, there were four factors for industrial location: two regional factors, transport and labor costs, and two local factors: agglomerating and deglomerating forces. He also mentioned the natural and social factors, however, these factors were ignored in his research (Smith, 1981; Tong, 1979)

Weber tried to answer the question of where production will take place, given the price and location of the materials and the position of the market. Tord Paladeder, in 1935, revised, and edited Weber's research and expanded it by analyzing the extent to which price effect the area in which a producer could sell his goods, given: the place of

62

production, the competitive conditions, factory costs, and transportation rates (McPherson, 1995; Smith, 1981).

Table 3 summarizes the specific location factors that theorists considered in their research. This table does not include all of the location theorists in the literature. However, contributors that had different approaches are selected to understand broader aspects of the literature.

After Weber (1909), Edgar Hoover (1937) included both demand and institutional factors in his analysis. However, he did not attempt to develop a static theoretical model that would predict the location of industry (McPherson, 1995; Smith, 1981; Tong, 1979)

August Loesch, in 1940, stated that market demand and the sales potential were the critical factors that were not taken into account by the earliest economists. He then used the demand as the major variable in the development of a location theory. Instead of concentrating on the least cost or the maximum revenue, he chose to find the place of maximum profits, where total revenue exceeded total cost by the greatest amount (Tong, 1979).

George Renner, in 1947, was the first person who stated his ideas as general principles. He made geographers more aware of the relevant works of economists. The location factors that he considered are shown in Table 3 (Tong, 1979).

Another theorist, Melvin L. Greenhut (1956-1963), was a well-known researcher in the field of spatial economics. He asserted that demand should be considered as a major location variable. He defined demand with six items (Tong, 1979, pg.24).

1. The shape of the demand curve for a given product
2. The location of competitors, which in turn partially determines
   a. The magnitude of the demand, and
   b. The cross-elasticity of demand at different places
3. The significance of proximity, type of service, and speed of service; prejudices of consumers
4. The relationship between personal contacts and sales

Table 3 Location factors considered by different theorists (McPherson, 1995; Smith, 1981; Tong, 1979)

Researcher	Location Factors
Weber (1909)	1. General Regional Factors - Transportation factors - Labor Factors 2. General Local Factors - Agglomerating factors - Deglomerating fcators 3. Natural Factors 4. Social Factors
Edgar Hoover(1937)	1. Cost Factors Transportation costs at - procuring raw materials - distributing the finished product Production Costs(direct labor costs, administrative costs) - factor prices - quantities of factors needed for production 2. Natural factors
August Loesch (1940)	1. Transportation costs 2. Time costs 3. Selling costs 4. Business Risks 5. Climate, habit, income 6. Extent of business-plant expansion 7. Hindrance to trade 8. Entrepreneurial and managerial incompetence 9. Factor accesibility 10. Factor productivity 11. Tariffs 12. Human differences 13. Differences in politics 14. Reactions of other firms
Georg Renner (1947)	1. Raw Materials 2. Market 3. Labor 4. Power 5. Capital 6. Transportation
Melvin L. Greenhut (1956, 1963)	1. Cost of land 2. Cost of labor and management 3. Cost of materials and equipment 4. Cost of transportation 5. Personal factors
Walter Isard (1956,1960)	1.Transportation costs and certain other transfer costs 2. Cost associated with labor, power, taxes, insurance, interest, climate, topography, social and political media 3. The diverse elements which give rise to agglomeration and deglomeration economies

(Compiled by the author)

64

5. The extent of the market area, which itself is partially determined by cost factors and pricing policies
6. The competitiveness of the industry in location and price; certainty and uncertainty

This extensive definition of demand covers most of the important factors and is still valid today. In addition, he suggested a list of location factors that is presented in Table 3.[8] He was the first theorist who considered personal factors in his research.

Walter Isard (1956-1960) was the last location theorist who was recognized as a pioneering contributor to the evolving disciplines of regional science. However, he did not add much to the existing factors list. He classified factors differently than the other researchers (See Table 3).

Most location theories have some serious assumptions and only represent limited perspectives of the total picture (McPherson, 1995). However, they still have a great merit of forming a foundation to the empirical studies in terms of understanding the concept and generating a detailed location factors list.

Empirical Studies

Empirical studies on the topic of international investments (mainly plant location) started in the 1970s. Since this time significant amount of location factors have been grouped and discussed by numerous authors and researchers in different ways. The analysis of the empirical studies starts from the 'Fordist Mass Production Period' and continues with 'Information and Communication Period' and 'Globalization Period' (See Figure 12).

Fordist Mass Production (1930s-1980s)

During the Fordist Mass Production period (1930s-1980s), most of the researches were about either plant location decisions for domestic companies in the US, or plant

---

[8] See Tong (1979) for details

location decisions for foreign companies in the US. In this period, Tong (1979) published his book, *Plant Location Decisions of Foreign Manufacturing Investors*. He applied a survey with a detailed location factors list to the foreign manufacturing investors in the US (See Appendix A). His list has some location factors, which are specifically applicable to the US, such as state tax rates and local tax rates, and some factors which are not applicable to a third world country during that period, such as education facilities, availability of managerial and technical personnel, etc. However, overall, data for the location factors were elaborately collected in accordance with the demands of that period of time.

Information & Communication (1980s-1990s)

Several surveys were conducted to determine the importance of the location factors for specifically managers and employers in a company, and for the company itself (Hayter, 1997; Schmenner, 1982; Tong, 1979). Between 1982 and 1990, four North American surveys were conducted with high technology companies (Hayter, 1997)[9]: a) Joint Economic Congress (US) Survey (1982), b) Office of Technology Assessment (US) Survey (1984), c) Christy and Ironside's Alberta Survey (1987), and d) Bathelt and Hecht's Ontario Survey (1990) Results from these surveys proved the impact of industry type on the importance of the location factors. Skilled labor factor was in the first and second places in the surveys as expected. However, other factors were ranked differently. This study showed that the ranks or importance of the location factors might differ according to the industry in which a company operates.

---

[9] See Appendix A for a detail list of location factors.

Watts (1987) on the other hand, carried out a survey for secondary plants in North Carolina. This survey confirmed the wide range of location factors relevant to the location of branch plants (Hayter, 1997; Watts, 1987).[10]

Hunt and Koulamas (1989) applied a narrower list than the other researchers. In their list, factors were receptive national government, number of permits needed, time to obtain permits, large number of possible sites to choose from, large enough work force, educational levels of work force and low/stable inflation rate (Hunt & Koulamas, 1989). This list mostly concentrates on the permits for location in other countries. Other than this focus, only labor and economic factors are inserted in the survey, which is not enough for an international investment analysis.

During this period, only Hax and Majluf (1983) and Hunt and Koulamas (1989) conducted their research on a global basis whereas, other researchers only considered the domestic location of plants, R&D facilities and other facilities.

Until 1990s, the effect of domestic location or foreign investors' location in the US was dominant. Several surveys were conducted to determine the importance of the location factors for specific managers and employers in a company, and for the company itself in the US. Tong (1979), Schmenner (1982) and other studies that are cited in Hayter's book, *The Dynamics of Industrial Location:The Factory, The Firm, The Production System* are selected examples from the literature (Hayter, 1997; Schmenner, 1982; Tong, 1979).

Globalization (1990s- present)

The wave of domestic plant location has disappeared with the globalization era. Companies have started thinking internationally. New location factors emerged in the surveys, such as, regional trade barriers and international concerns. In 1995, Badri,

---

[10] See Appendix A for a detail list of location factors.

Davis and Davis, designed an explanatory study of the industrial location decision behavior of executives. They established procedures for classifying manufacturers located in other sites worldwide into groups on the basis of their scores on the same variables of the same location analysis. A detailed location factors list was applied under the categories of:

- transportation related factors,
- labor related factors,
- raw materials related factors,
- market related factors,
- industrial site related factors,
- utilities related factors,
- government attitude related factors,
- tax structure related factors,
- climate related factors community related factors,
- political situation of foreign country related factors,
- global competition and survival related factors,
- government regulation related factors and
- economic related factors (Badri, Davis, & Davis, 1995) [11].

This extensive list covers virtually all of the location factors that should appear in today's list.

Yurimoto and Masui (1995), made a valuable contribution to the decision-making process for investment decisions. They identified the location factors and assigned evaluation indices for each factor that helped quantify the qualitative data. This assignment gave a clearer picture about these factors. Then, they developed a decision support system to evaluate and select the countries (Yurimoto & Masui, 1995).

---

[11] See Appendix A for more details.

Ulgado (1996) categorized the location factors as: local and labor attitudes, community environment, incentives, land and transportation services, international concerns, synergy logistics, input logistics, capital concerns, market logistics, skilled human resource availability and tax rates. Different location attributes were examined under each factor category for US and foreign companies (Ulgado, 1996).

During the globalization era, multinational companies emerged. Vos (1997) concentrated on this type of company, and proposed a design method to structure and support their international manufacturing and logistics structure. His list of location factors were: supply of materials, labor, capital, energy, distribution, technology intensity, control intensity (respective labor requirements/total labor requirements), labor to capital ratio, and value density (Vos, 1997). This research interrogates the decision of locating an additional capacity, if plant location will be a solution to the problem in the identification stage or not. After this decision, the system evaluates countries according to the different factors identified by the model.

Brush, Maritan and Karnani (1999) developed a framework and empirically investigated the combined importance of international business and manufacturing strategy literature for the plant location choice of multinational firms. They defined manufacturing strategy as the choice between locating an independent versus an integrated plant. The location factors that they considered were: proximity to downstream nodes, proximity to upstream nodes, access to raw materials and energy, access to capital and local technology, access to skilled labor, access to low cost labor, government policies, societal characteristics, and regulation (Brush et al., 1999). In this case, it seems that their concentration was on both the country selection and the site selection. A categorization of the factors might be useful according to the different levels in the decision-making.

MacCarty and Atthirawong (2001) investigated critical factors in international location decisions from the real world situation. They claim that in their future research, they are planning to use Delphi method to structure the important factors according to the type of business, size of business, location of parent company, and geographical areas. (MacCarty & Atthirawong, 2001)

Consequently, different location factors were evaluated to apprehend certain recurring location factors and their influence on location problems. Researchers concentrated on specific samples and developed the location factors list according to their own samples. Therefore, a more comprehensive list is necessary for practical applications. A categorization of these factors would also help the decision maker do the analysis of investments more easily.

A COMPREHENSIVE LOCATION FACTORS LIST FOR INTERNATIONAL INVESTMENTS

A list of 49 factors was developed with the aid of the literature survey, interviews with companies[12], the experience of the university professors and the consulting experience of the author. Seven categories were determined:

- Cost
- Availability
- Accessibility
- Quality
- Risk/Uncertainty
- Ease of Operations
- Quality of life

Each category is analyzed and definitions of the factors are presented as follows:

Cost

The factors under this category are listed in Table 4. There are two types of factors in this category. The first type has a direct effect on the cost of the product and these factors are 'total cost of the product', 'cost of quota', 'tax rates' and 'transaction

---

[12] Interviews were conducted to validate the instrument not to gather statistical data.

costs'. The second type of cost factors: 'participation in economic trade groups', 'government incentives', and 'cost of land' has an indirect effect on the overall cost.

'Total cost of product' represents the landing cost of the product to the desired destination. It includes raw material cost, labor cost, utilities cost, transportation cost and other costs related to manufacturing. At the beginning of this research, each factor listed under the 'Total cost of product' factor was considered separately. However, after the interviews with representatives within the US textile and apparel industry, it is understood that nowadays, companies are primarily interested in the total cost of the product. On the contrary to the past practices of considering only the labor costs, most of the interviewees mentioned that they were considering every piece of the total cost of production and comparing countries based on one figure, 'total cost of product'. Therefore, all of the mentioned costs are aggregated under the 'total cost of product' factor.

'Cost of Quota' is the second direct cost factor in the list. This is the price that manufacturers pay to secure quotas in those exporting countries in which quota allocations are openly bought and sold (Dickerson, 1999). This cost is attributed to the total cost of the product in the applicable countries. With the reduction of quotas among World Trade Organization (WTO) countries, this factor will lose its importance for them; however, it will remain important for third world countries who are not a WTO member yet.

The third direct factor is the 'tax rate'. Tax is a fee charged by a government on a product, income, or activity[13]. Tariff is a special tax on imported goods (Dickerson, 1999). So, tax rate is also an additional cost over the total cost of the product imposed by the government. If a company wants to produce in another country, it has to pay a tax to that country. If the same company wants to export the goods to another country,

---

[13] http://www.investorwords.com/cgi-bin/getword.cgi?4879

71

it has to pay a tariff for the imported goods. This factor, thus, encompasses both of the above taxes and any other taxes that may be associated with transactions. 'Tax rate' might be more important after the elimination of the quotas. It may be used to counteract reduced quotas in effort to control trade.

'Transaction costs', the fourth direct cost factor, are the costs associated with discovering prices, undertaking negotiations, drawing up contracts, and settling disputes. Any agent fees and other middle tier costs are also included in this factor.

The first indirect factor is 'Participation in economic trade groups'. Trade groups are sets of countries participating in a special trade relationship that encourages and facilitates trade within the region (Dickerson, 1999). Participation in a trade group provides advantages on cost related factors. Examples of these groups are North American Free Trade Agreement (NAFTA) and European Union (EU) as regional blocs.

Table 4 Cost factors

Direct Cost Factors	Indirect Cost Factors
Total Cost of Product	Participation in International Economic Trading Group
Cost of Quota	Cost of land
Tax Rates	Government Incentives
Transaction Costs	

'Cost of land' is the second indirect factor. This cost is mainly for plant location decisions. For any other type of international investments, this cost factor has a minimal effect. 'Cost of land' can include the property taxes and fees to agents for acquisitions.

'Government incentives' is the third indirect factor in the list. It includes tax credits, utility savings, and other economic benefits for businesses to locate, relocate or expand in certain areas. The term may be also known as empowerment zones, 'economic development or 'enterprise trading zones'[14].

---

[14] New York Small Business Resource Center

Availability

This section questions the availability of various factors in the candidate country. These factors are listed in Table 5. Most of them are self-explanatory and only the ones that were found to be vague are explained below:

In the 'availability of skilled labor' factor, skilled labor represents the labor force with the minimum required skill to satisfactorily perform the necessary processes like sewing. They should not require additional training to do these processes.

Table 5 Availability factors

Availability of Skilled Labor	Availability of Suppliers
Bargaining Power of Suppliers	Availability of Raw Materials
Availability of Lending Institutions	Availability of Technology
Availability of Transportation Modes	Availability of Capital
Availability of Middle Management	Availability of Infrastructure
Availability of New Markets	Availability of Government Incentives

'Bargaining power of suppliers' factor is imported to the list from Porter's Five Forces Model (Porter, 1980). In that model, Porter discusses the situations when suppliers can be powerful, and if that would be the case, when suppliers can squeeze the profits of the companies by increasing price. So, this factor questions if there is such a power in the candidate country or not.

'Availability of lending institutions' factor questions the availability of the banks or other institutions to lend/transfer money in the candidate country. This factor is important since it inherently reflects the financial situation in the country and the rules of the country in terms of borrowing and lending. If a company does not have sufficient funding for international investment, it can borrow money from the institutions in the

(http://www2.nypl.org/smallbiz/business/locating/locating_location.htm)

candidate country, or for some cases, it may be more profitable to use the candidate country's money.

'Availability of middle management' factor is also an important factor for international investments. Labor is not the only component that is needed to run a manufacturing facility, it may be more critical to find the right people to manage the labor in a plant, especially when nobody wants to relocate to the selected location from the parent company's hometown.

Accessibility

This group questions the accessibility of the factors that are important for manufacturing. 'Lead time' represents the total time including the manufacturing and the transportation of the goods to the desired location (e.g. port, airport). The accessibility of the markets and suppliers are also questioned with 'Proximity to markets' and 'Proximity to suppliers' factors. 'Flexibility of the production' is about the capabilities of the companies in the candidate country. This factor asks if companies in general are accessible for different types of products within a product category. The demographics of the production in terms of location, size, and age of the industry is questioned with 'Local integration between fabric and garment manufacturers' factor.

Table 6 Accessibility factors

Lead Time
Proximity to Markets
Proximity of Suppliers
Flexibility of the Production
Local Integration between fabric and garment manufacturers

Quality

The quality group incorporates three important factors and most of the companies interviewed consider all of these three factors as a given. However, the author still took these factors into consideration since the interviewed companies do not represent the whole population.

Table 7 Quality factors

Quality of the Product
Ethical Standards
Environmental Standards

Risk / Uncertainty

The fifth group of factors is risk/uncertainty group. Factors that incorporate risk are listed in Table 8. The trends in most of the factors and the degree of stability in the country from different aspects are considered.

'Political stability', for example, represents a country's situation in its political arena. Whether the party in charge is supported by the majority of the population in one country, or there is a chance of early elections due to illegal or criminal actions of the party, or there is a bias of the in charge party towards religious action or communist action are some questions that can be asked to evaluate the political stability in the country. An unstable environment can cause risk in terms of trade and this can influence the investments in a country since rules may change due to a change in the policy makers' actions. Political objectives of a country have affected the US textile and apparel trade policies. For example, although Cuba has the potential to become a critical apparel production site, trade with the US is prohibited because of US opposition to Fidel Castro's communist rule (Dickerson, 1999).

75

'Banking system stability' may cause similar effects as the 'political stability' factor in the financial arena. The banking system structure of a country is one of the indicators of its financial position. If it is not well developed, it may cause fluctuations in the interest rates, inflation rates, exchange rates, etc.

This section implicitly covers the future expectations (time factor in international investments) of the companies. For example, if a country is currently unstable but forecasts for indicators for ten years appear to be good, a company may consider a country with a medium level of stability.

Table 8 Risk/uncertainty factors

Labor Unions	Banking System Stability
Income Trends	Interest Rate
Population Trends	Inflation Rate
Location of Competitors	Delivery Reliability
Political Stability	National Content Laws of the Countries
Currency Stability	

'National content laws of the countries' is the last factor in the list. This factor questions if a country has specific rules for hazardous chemicals or other additives that may be used in the textile or apparel industry. A difference in these rules may cause risk for a company in an international operation.

Ease of Operations

This group examines the level of complexity of doing business in the candidate country, and includes legal rules about investments, strategic partnerships, imports and exports, and other legal laws (listed in Table 9).

Table 9 Ease of operation factors

Participation in International Economic Trading Group
Clarity of Corporate Investment Rules
Regulations concerning Joint Ventures and Mergers
Taxation of Foreign-owned Companies
Favorable Ownership Rights
Favorable Legal Systems
Favorable Import/Export Regulations

'Clarity of corporate investment rules' can ease the operations for an investor. If there are clear rules and clear ways to reach these rules, investors can easily conduct their investments according to the specified rules. On the contrary, if there is nothing in terms of investment rules or they are not clear enough, investors may encounter several problems after conducting the investment.

The same situation is applicable to the 'regulations concerning joint ventures and mergers' factor. Companies should know before conducting the investment if there are specific regulations that can impede operations and rights of the foreign investor. On the other hand, there may be 'favorable ownership right' in a country. Country can give more privileges if you totally own the site rather than you own 50% of it.

In conclusion, all of the factors in this section either eases or hinders the operations in a specified country. Therefore, companies should be aware of these factors for international investment.

Quality of Life

Four factors in Table 10 represent the quality of life in the candidate country. This group is mostly important for companies that consider plant location for international investment. It is also important to some extent for strategic partnership investments.

Table 10 Quality of life factors

Availability of universities, colleges, schools
Cost of Living
Size of per capita income
Monthly Average Temperature

DISCUSSION & CONCLUSIONS

Starting from 1909, different location factors have been analyzed by researchers. Literature survey showed that several location factors gained and lost their importance during the different periods of time. Considering important periods in the history, these factors were determined and examined and major findings were extracted from the literature.

The major finding from the literature review is that different factors were considered as important according to the different periods. For example, cost factors were not the most important factors in the past since the only consideration of companies was a new investment in the US. Costs were not that much different from each other. However, nowadays, the most important factors are cost factors. Another important factor today is the trade agreements for the US textile and apparel industry, which was not even in the list of the location factors in the past. So, it was essential to come up with an extensive list of location factors.

A list of 49 factors was developed with the aid of the literature survey, the interviews with companies, the experience of the university professors and the consulting experience of the author. Seven groups are formed to categorize these factors. This comprehensive list was formed according to today's needs after analyzing the environment from different perspectives. The validation of the list was performed during the interviews. However, there are limitations of the study. The dynamics for international investments are changing so fast. New factors may appear that are not considered in this list. Additionally, some factors may be very broad for companies and they may want to add a specific factor as a separate one to the list. This limitation was encountered during the interviews with industry people. They came up with different factors and realized that the specific factors that they were mentioned were under a factor in the list.

This comprehensive list can be used as a tool during international investment analysis. Companies can review the list and rate countries based on their performances in the factors.

A suggestion for future work is to categorize the location factors based on companies' internal environment. This paper presented the comprehensive list, however, most of the time, companies do not considered every factor in the list with the same importance and based on their preferences the list can be narrowed down. The process and the factors that affect this process can be analyzed as a future work.

.

REFERENCES

Badri, M. A., Davis, D. L., & Davis, D. (1995). Decision Support Models for the Location of Firms in Industrial Sites. International Journal of Operations & Production Management, 15(1), 50-62.

Brush, T. H., Maritan, C. A., & Karnani, A. (1999). The Plant Location Decision in Multinational Manufacturing Firms:An Emprical Analysis of International Business and Manufacturing Strategy Perspectives. Production and Operations Management, 8(2), 109-132.

Notes on Facility Location. (1989). Harvard Business College

Dickerson, K. (1999). Textiles and apparel in the global economy. New Jersey: Prentice-Hall, Inc.

Hax, A., & Majluf, S. (1983). The Industry Attractiveness-Business Strength Matrix in Strategic Planning. Interfaces, 13(April), 54-71.

Hayter, R. (1997). The Dynamics of Industrial Location:The Factory, The Firm, The Production System. England: John Wiley & Sons.

Hunt, J. R., & Koulamas, C. P. (1989). A Model for Evaluating Potential Facility Locations on a Global Basis. SAM Advanced Management Journal(Summer), 19-23.

Isard, W. (1956). Location and Space-Economy. New York: The MIT Press.

MacCarty, B., & Atthirawong, W. (2001). Critical Factors in International Location Decisions: A Delphi study. Paper presented at the Twelfth Annual Conference of the Production and Operations Management Society, Orlando, FL.

McPherson, E. M. (1995). Plant Location Selection Techniques. New Jersey: Noyes Publications.

Porter, M. (1980). Competitive Strategy Techniques for analyzing industries and competitors. New York: The Free Press.

Schmenner, R. W. (1982). Making Business Location Decisions: Prentice-Hall.

Smith, D. M. (1981). Industrial Location: An economic geographical analysis (second edition ed.). New York: John Wiley&Sons, Inc.

Tong, H.-M. (1979). Plant Location Decision of Foreign Manufacturing Investors. Michigan: UMI Research Press.

Ulgado, F. M. (1996). Location Characteristics of Manufacturing Investments in the US: A Comparison of American and Foreign-based Firms. Management International Review, 36(1), 7-24.

Vos, B. (1997). Redesigning International Manufacturing and Logistics Structures. International Journal of Physical Distribution & Logistics Management, 27(7), 377-394.

Watts, H. (1987). Industrial Geography. New York: Wiley.

Weber, A. (1929). Theory of the Location of Industries. New York: Russell&Russell.

Yurimoto, S., & Masui, T. (1995). Design of a decision support system for overseas plant location in the EC. International Journal of Production Economics, 41, 411-418.

PART IV: A COMPREHENSIVE INSTRUMENT FOR CUSTOMIZED INVESTMENT DECISIONS IN THE GLOBAL ARENA

INTRODUCTION

Companies invest internationally to utilize the comparative advantages among different countries (Camuffo et al., 2001; Dunning, 1988; Murray & Kotabe, 1999). Investment strategies range from the formation of strategic partnership with local companies to owning a plant in the selected country. Today, with the effect of increased dynamics in the environment, strategic partnerships (e.g., mergers, acquisitions) appear as a strong alternative for plant location decisions.

Investment decisions have been vital for companies since they require a high commitment, in terms of both capital and human resources. For this critical decision, the traditional decision-making process encompasses three stages.

1. Determination of the candidate countries is the first stage.
2. These countries are then evaluated, during stage two, based on a list of location factors, which are identified by the company. In most of the cases, the same list of factors is considered for different types of companies and for different types of plant location decisions.
3. The decision-making process ends with the analysis of the countries. Stage three is the final decision making. The final decision is given after the analysis.

This three-step decision-making process, however, has serious flaws. The heart of the process is the second stage where companies select the important location factors to evaluate candidate countries. To emphasize the importance of this step, it can be said that the decision-making process can be defined as selecting the right location factors based on a company's needs. The traditional way, explained in the above paragraph, puts no extra attention on that step. However, this decision-making process can differ based on the organizational culture of the company. A specific organizational value or belief, which may be unique to one company, could shape the process in various ways. Many researchers examined this issue implicitly by comparing foreign and domestic

84

countries in their research (Hax & Majluf, 1983; Hunt & Koulamas, 1989; Tong, 1979). In addition to values and beliefs, the strategic approach of companies has a serious effect on the process. Companies pursue different strategies depending on characteristics of the markets and products involved (Brush, 1999). The weight the location factors and/or the list of location factors changes based on the strategic practices of the companies. The process also changes according to the product type and the sector type, and the results from several surveys have proved the impact of industry type on the importance of the location factors (Hayter, 1997).

This paper presents a comprehensive instrument for investment decisions. This novel approach is built upon four main pillars: the strategy of the company, the organizational culture of the company, the sector where the company operates, and the role of external environment. The instrument was developed to guide the companies to an effective customization of the location factors and of their priorities according to companies' needs.

LITERATURE REVIEW

Empirical studies about investment decisions started in 1970s. From this period, significant amounts of location factors have been grouped and discussed by numerous authors and researchers in different ways. The literature is examined to find out the different dimensions[15] used for investment decisions in research.

The most common dimension in surveys is the *location* of the parent company. The location of the parent company directly affects the organizational culture. Different organizational cultures influences the decision making process for investment decisions and researchers have conducted studies to understand these different decision making behaviors. In 1979, Tong applied a survey with a detailed location factors list to the foreign manufacturing investors in the US. In Ulgado's (1996) research, different

---

[15] Dimension refers to the different aspects that researchers use to analyze the nature of the problem.

location attributes were examined for US and foreign companies (Ulgado, 1996). Brush, Maritan & Karnani (1999) also analyzed foreign and domestic companies in their research. Another study with a sample of 2705 international plant location decisions was conducted by Henisz and Delios (2001) for Japanese multinational corporations. In a Delphi study, MacCarty and Atthirawong (2001) used location of the manufacturing plant and of the parent company as one of the dimensions for their instrument. In all of the aforementioned studies, the differences in the decision-making behavior of companies were analyzed and results are driven by consideration of the origin of the companies, in other words, the organizational culture of the companies.

The industry/sector type is the second most common dimension in the literature and many researchers examined the different weighting of this location factor based on the industry type of the companies. Between 1982 and 1990, four North American surveys (Joint Economic Congress (US) Survey (1982), Office of Technology Assessment (US) Survey (1984), Christy and Ironside's Alberta Survey (1987), and Bathelt and Hecht's Ontario Survey (1990) were conducted for high technology companies (Hayter, 1997). The president and fellows of Harvard College considered the list of factors affecting facility location decisions as relatively constant, however, they argued the importance or weighting of the factors could vary greatly by industry, product life cycle and facility type (Notes on Facility, 1989). In 1995, Badri, Davis & Davis, designed an explanatory study as an investigation of the industrial location decision behavior of executives. Ulgado (1996) also considered the industry effect in comparing domestic and foreign firms' important location factors lists. MacCarthy et.al. (2001) considered types of businesses as a factor where firms located.

Three additional dimensions were found in the literature besides "location"[16] (Henisz & Delios, 2001):

---

[16] See above paragraph for details about 'location' dimension.

86

- "Imitation" refers to copy the behavior of the other companies, in other words giving investment decisions based on the previous experiences of competitor companies.
- "Policy uncertainty" in a country deters investment. "When a firm is uncertain about future regulations, rates of taxation, or even macroeconomic policies, it is less likely to make long-term capital investments".
- "Firm specific uncertainty" refers to the level of previous experience of the firm in the selected country.

In a Delphi study (MacCarty & Atthirawong, 2001), "nature of the business" was used as an additional dimension, where nature of business refers to the organizational characteristics of the companies, such as world class manufacturing company, large company, and medium-size company .

Brush, Maritan and Karnani (1999) used "manufacturing strategy" as one of their dimensions. It is defined by two factors: the degree of integration and the location relative to parent headquarters. "Integration was measured along two dimensions: the degree of managerial coordination between the plant and the rest of the business unit and the presence of material flows between the plant and other plants in the business units." (Brush et al., 1999). Another dimension that they used is "the age of the company". This dimension resembles the "firm specific uncertainty" dimension mentioned above. Both of the dimensions question the experience of the company. The dimensions are summarized in Table 11.

New studies proved that all of these dimensions had an effect in the investment behaviors of the companies. However, not all of the dimensions are considered in the literature. In most cases, one or two-dimensional analysis were conducted in detail. This paper offers a more comprehensive approach for global investments than the existing ones because of the inclusion of multi-dimensions in the instrument development.

Table 11 Summary of the dimensions for investment decisions

Dimension[17]	Description	Researcher
Location	Host company location, parent company location	Tong (1979) Ulgado (1996) Brush, Maritan and Karnani (1999) Henisz and Delios (2001) MacCarty and Atthirawong (2001)
Industry/sector type	Sector type which firms located	Hayter (1997) College(1989) Badri, Davis and Davis(1995) Ulgado (1996) MacCarthy et al.(2001)
Imitation	Imitation of the other firms	Henisz and Delios (2001)
Uncertainty	Policy uncertainty, firm specific uncertainty	Henisz and Delios (2001)
Nature of the business	World class manufacturing, large company, medium sized company, etc.	MacCarty and Atthirawong (2001)
Manufacturing strategy	Degree of integration, location relative to parent headquarters	Brush, Maritan and Karnani (1999)
Age of the organization	Younger than ten years, older than ten years	Brush, Maritan and Karnani (1999)

CONCEPTUAL FRAMEWORK

The literature review revealed the fact that the decision-making process for global investments is a multi-dimensional process. However, the dimensions that were analyzed in the literature were multi-level. Sometimes, researchers concentrated on micro-level dimensions, sometimes, they analyzed companies using macro-level dimensions. The dimensions listed in Table 11 represent a summary of the major dimensions both in macro- and micro-levels.

In this study, dimensions in the literature (summarized in Table 11) are analyzed and grouped under four macro level dimensions. These groupings are performed based on the literature review, and consulting experience of the author. A field test was conducted with an executive from a leading apparel company after completing the draft

---

[17] The definitions of the dimensions are given in the text.

of the instrument. Additions were incorporated to the dimensions after this field test[18]. The list is also validated by speaking to the faculty experts. The derivation of the macro level categories is shown in Table 12.

Table 12 Derivation of the macro level dimensions

Group	Dimension	Description
Strategy of the company	1. Manufacturing strategy	1. Degree of integration, location relative to parent headquarters
Organizational culture of the company	1. Imitation 2. Location 3. Nature of the business 4. Age of the organization 5. Uncertainty	1. Imitation of the other firms 2. Host company location, parent company location 3. World class manufacturing, large company, medium sized company, etc. 4. Younger than ten years, older than ten years 5. Policy uncertainty, firm specific uncertainty
Sector of the company	1. Industry/sector type	1. Sector type which firms located
External environment of the company	1. Uncertainty	1. Policy uncertainty, firm specific uncertainty

So, the following macro dimensions are defined for the instrument:

➤ Strategy of the Company
➤ Organizational Culture of the Company
➤ Sector of the Company
➤ External Environment of the Company

The conceptual framework is depicted in Figure 13 using the above dimensions.

---

[18] Details will be discussed in the following section.

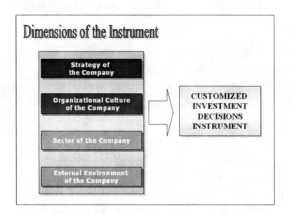

Figure 13 Conceptual framework

These dimensions represent the company as a whole. Strategic approach, organizational culture and sector type characterize the internal environment of the company, whereas sector type and other issues in the external environment form the global field in which company operates (Figure 14). The dimensions are examined under these two categorizations: internal environment and external environment as follows.

Figure 14 Categorization of the factors

Internal Environment

The internal environment defines the actions of the company in this challenging environment. The main factors that affect these actions are the strategic approach of the company, the organizational culture in the company and the sector type of the company (Figure 14).

Strategic Approach

A country's specific advantage over other countries is called the comparative advantage of that country. Advantages in cost figures, legal regulations, economic stability, etc. of a country would be considered as comparative advantages for that country. In that, a company's desire to benefit from the comparative advantages of the countries forms the basis for global investment decisions. They are prone to locate activities in other nations not only to tap local cost advantages but additionally, to perform R&D, gain access to specialized local skills, gain access to other markets, or develop relationships with pivotal customers (Porter, 1990).

On the other hand, companies try to create competitive advantages[19] over other companies to survive in the global marketplace. One way of creating a competitive advantage is using countries' comparative advantages. Porter (1998) states the ability to shift from comparative advantage to competitive advantage as the basic challenge for companies. For the textile and apparel industry, this shift is even harder. Nowadays, trade agreements make it possible for almost every company in the world to reach out to any place and conduct operations. Comparative advantages like low cost figures and availability of unskilled labor no longer confer competitive advantage to the companies. Therefore, textile and apparel companies have to determine their own strategic approaches/objectives and move towards these targets. They have to advance beyond

---

[19] Competitive advantage refers to the advantage that enables a firm to beat its competition in the marketplace (Dickerson, 1999).

the traditional location selection and have to consider each country's comparative advantages as a chance to create a competitive advantage in line with their strategic approach. Hunt and Koulamas (1989) stated that the move, theoretically, should be made with strategic considerations with respect to both present and future needs of the company. The objectives of the move should be consistent with and assumed under either: the corporate objectives or divisional objectives developed during the planning process (Hunt & Koulamas, 1989). In this respect, Ietto_gillies (2000) asks if operating across many nation-states gives advantages that can not be achieved by operating across many regions (Ietto_gillies, 2000). The answer totally depends whether the companies are evaluating their self-interests and objectives well enough so that they can evaluate different locations considering their own interests. Thus, companies should act after deciding the ways of gaining benefits from the comparative advantages of the countries and turning these benefits into competitive advantages for themselves.

The empirical studies in the literature mostly concentrated on the manufacturing strategies of the companies. However, above-mentioned reasons prove that a more general approach is important to start to generate valid competitive advantages for companies. So, strategic approach of a company is one of the main dimensions that companies have to consider before making any investment decisions.

Organizational Culture

Cox (1993) defined organizational culture as "underlying values, beliefs and principles that serve as a foundation for the organization's management system, as well as the set of management practices and behaviors that both exemplify and reinforce those principles" (Cox, 1993). Companies' management systems differ from each other based on their organizational culture and this difference also affects the decision-making process of the companies. Based on their specific organizational values/principles, companies make the decision of selecting the right country to operate.

In the literature, this dimension is analyzed by using variables that influence the organizational culture of the companies. In most cases, the effect of country culture was analyzed (e.g., Japan vs. USA). Imitation of the leader companies is another variable that represents the organizational culture of the companies since imitation would not be an option in any circumstances for some companies considering their organizational culture. An example would be small companies imitating the large corporations for their investment decisions e.g. to locate operations to the same area that large corporations are considering. Even large corporations can imitate companies in different stages of the product life cycle, e.g. Zara's imitation of designers to shorten the product development phase.

Nature of business (e.g., world-class corporation, medium sized company) is another variable that is discussed in the literature. In accordance with the above examples, it is clear that there can be distinct differences when the size/nature of the company is concerned. This variable also shapes the organizational culture of the company. In addition, the age of the organization is another variable that is considered in the literature since the experience of the organization can be strength or threat for the organization, but it is definitely a variable in organizational culture of the organization.

Companies' response to the uncertainty in the environment is also a part of their organizational values and the degree of risk taking for the company is critical for most of the investment decisions.

After analyzing all of the above variables, "organizational culture" is considered as a macro-level dimension in this instrument. The effect of organizational culture can sometimes be a clear-cut for most of the investment decisions. For example, if there is a value of quick response in terms of customer satisfaction in the organizational culture of a company, it will prefer being close to the customers. Therefore, countries could be cut from the list if their proximities are not enough to satisfy this value of the organization.

93

For most of the US textile companies, this example can be valid since their customers (the US apparel companies) have moved their operations to overseas. They are forced to move to overseas, to satisfy and not to lose their customers, or they are forced to create different competitive advantages to compete with the overseas production. Thus, the response of the organizations to the uncertainty of the environment with their organizational culture is critical for the US textile companies.

Sector of the Company

With the aid of the literature review and the field test, "Sector of the company" is determined as another important macro-level dimension for the instrument. It refers to the business sector in which the company operates, such as, being a textile or an apparel company.

"The commodity chain for apparel extends from the upstream sectors that supply the garment industry with its raw materials and intermediate products-the fiber and textile industries- to the downstream sectors that manage the distribution of finished apparel including marketing and retail. Sectors at both ends of the chain tend to be characterized by more advanced technology and greater capital intensity than are associated with the production of garments" (Bair & Gereffi, 2002)

In the field test, the executive of a leading apparel company emphasized the importance of the sector type and mentioned that all of the preferences would change based on the sector of the company. The priorities of a textile company would differ from an apparel company, or a nonwoven company considering their markets, their way of doing business, and their investment structures. This valuable comment validated the results of the empirical studies in the literature. Thus, "sector of the company" is included in the instrument.

External Environment

Sector of the Company

"Sector of the company" has been previously discussed in the internal environment; however, the same variable has also an effect in the external environment of the company. Competitors' actions/decisions change the market dynamics and companies may have to make decisions to respond to these changing dynamics. The changes may be different from one sector to another. One sector may be very competitive; the other one may be dominated by couple of major players only. In those types of situations, organizations have to make actions considering their own external environment.

External Environment of the Company

Dynamics of the environment is continuously changing and nowadays uncertainty is a big factor in decision-making models. Risk management has become an ongoing process in the organizations. Investment decisions embody a high amount of risk, especially textile investments due to their nature of high investments in dollars. Therefore, companies have to be aware of the current happenings in economic, political, sociological and technological environment. Threats like SARS or terrorism, and opportunities like trade agreements affect daily decisions in textile and apparel industry. Companies try to direct their operations into other countries after analyzing these types of threats and opportunities in the environment. Trade agreements play a particularly important role for the textile and apparel industry. These agreements affect the location of global investment since quotas and tariffs comprise a significant amount in the cost structure. As a result, "external environment of the company" is considered as a macro-level dimension in the instrument.

CUSTOMIZED INVESTMENT DECISIONS INSTRUMENT

Based on the conceptual framework (Figure 13), an instrument was developed to reveal the decision-making behavior[20] of companies considering their strategy, organizational culture, sector and the external environment in which they operate. Variables were identified to represent each macro-level dimension. The variables are depicted in Figure 15.

There are five sections in the instrument:

- ➢ Strategic Approach of the Company
- ➢ Important Statistics
- ➢ Importance of Location Factors
  - Product Type
  - List of location factors
- ➢ Company Profile
- ➢ User Profile

The first section of the instrument is the strategic approach of the company. This section contains three parts:

- ➢ Investment Decisions
- ➢ Corporate Strategy
- ➢ Organizational Approach

The questions address the strategic preferences of the company, the growth strategy of the company, the product strategy of the company and the organizational culture in the company. The 'strategic approach' questions were adapted from Porter (1980), and Higgins & Vincze (1993). The questions about organizational culture of the company were adapted from Andrews (1995)(Andrews, 1995; Higgins & Vincze, 1993; Porter, 1980).

---

[20] Decision making behavior of a company represents the selection of the location factors

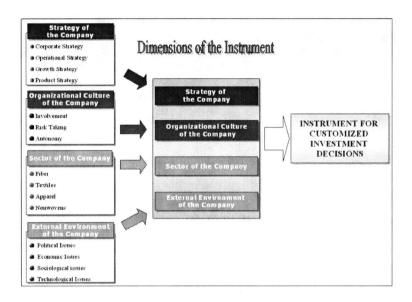

Figure 15 The structure of the instrument

The second section is the "Important Statistics" section. This section questions the important statistic that companies consider in plant location decisions. The third section is the importance of location factors section. This list is adapted from the literature review about plant location factors[21]. The last two sections are about company profiles and user profiles and are developed using personal experience. The relationship of the variables with the instrument items is depicted in Table 13.

---

[21] The literature review of location factors is Section 2.4 in this document.

Table 13 Instrument items related to macro-level dimensions

Dimension	Variable	Instrument Item	Level of Data
Strategy of the Company	➢ Corporate Strategy ➢ Operational Strategy ➢ Growth Strategy ➢ Product Strategy	Q1 Q3 Q4 Q5 Q6 Q7 Q8 Q2 Q16 Q17 Q18 Q23 Q24 Q25	Nominal Nominal Nominal Nominal Nominal Nominal Nominal Rank Order Interval Interval Nominal Nominal Nominal
Organizational Culture of the Company	➢ Involvement ➢ Risk Taking ➢ Autonomy	Q10 Q11 Q12 Q13 Q14 Q15 Q16 Q18	Nominal Nominal Nominal Nominal Nominal Nominal Interval Interval
Sector of the Company	➢ Fiber ➢ Textiles ➢ Apparel ➢ Nonwovens	Q16 Q18 Q21	Interval Interval Nominal
External Environment of the Company	➢ Political Issues ➢ Economic Issues ➢ Sociological Issues ➢ Technological Issues	Q16 Q18	Interval Interval

Definition of Variables

Strategic of the Company

Strategic approach of the company is characterized using four main areas:

- Corporate Strategy
- Specific Operational Strategy
- Product Strategy
- Growth Strategy

Corporate Strategy: Porter's generic business strategies were used to define the "Corporate Strategy" variable. According to Porter, there are three potentially successful generic strategies for companies (Porter, 1980):

- ✓ *Overall Cost Leadership*: Cost leadership requires cost minimization in virtually all areas. Efficiency should increase and cost reduction should be pursued vigorously to become the leader in the sector that company operates.
- ✓ *Differentiation*: The second generic strategy is differentiating the product or service of the firm, creating something that is perceived *industry wide* as being unique. Differentiation can be accomplished in any form like design or brand image, technology, customer service, etc.
- ✓ *Focus*: The final generic strategy is focusing on a particular buyer group, segment of the product line, or geographic market to serve a particular target very well.

Specific Operational Strategy: After questioning the macro level-corporate strategy, companies must be aware of their specific operational practices that serve to the generic corporate strategy. Generic strategies will be hard to pursue unless companies foster these strategies with operational level practices. These strategies are: Innovation, quality, continuous improvement, speed and flexibility (Higgins & Vincze, 1993). This variable is also addressed in the 'strategic approach of your company' section in the instrument.

Growth Strategy: Growth has four primary considerations:

- The type of growth (intensive, integrative or diversified growth),
- Its geographic focus (on regional, national or international markets),
- How it will take place (internally or externally through acquisitions, mergers, joint ventures or other alliances) and
- How quickly it will take place (Higgins & Vincze, 1993).

99

The aim in using this instrument is to understand the decision-making behavior of locating an operation in an international geographic location. This aim incorporated the type and geographic focus of the growth innately. How to grow is questioned in the 'strategic approach of your company' section and the speed of the growth is not taken into consideration in this instrument.

Product Strategy:

The textile and especially apparel industry include a wide variety of products. A field test for the instrument was conducted with an executive from a leading apparel company. The importance of product type is revealed based on the executive's comments on the questions in the instrument. The executive mentioned that not only the sector type but also the product type was important when considering which countries to make investment. He added that strategic objectives with a specific product type or product line were necessary to consider the locations appropriately. After this valuable comment, literature review regarding the classification of the product types was conducted.

After the literature review, four types of products are considered in the instrument. (Van Weele & Rozemeijer, ; Verra, 1999). These are:

- Strategic products
- Leverage products
- Routine products
- Bottleneck products

Strategic products are the products that can generate serious revenue for the company even if the percentage might be low in the overall product categories. Since the incorporation of these products in the total product mix can lead to significant profits, a well-conceived strategy is critical to gain the full potential of international investments. It is important to create a long-term relationship between the supplier and the company so that the company can work on improvements in the field of product quality, delivery reliability, product development and product design and cost reduction.

Strategic partnership with the suppliers is essential since there may not be plethora of supplier that can manufacture the strategic products. So, for this type of product, one can expect high profit, however, there is also a high risk when suppliers are concerned since they are not so many.

Leverage products represent products that can be manufactured by a large set of suppliers but have a large financial impact at the same time. Since the number of appropriate suppliers is high, companies have the power to force the supplier to offer the lowest price. So, this type of product can generate high profits and the supplier risk is very low since there are many suppliers.

Bottle neck products do not incorporate a strategic impact on financial results, however, a high supply risk is involved. Verra (1999) stated that there is the problem of disruption of supply, with heavy consequences for these products. Therefore everything should be done cautiously to secure supply (contracts with heavy penalties, safety stock, etc.) (Verra, 1999). So, this type of products has a high supplier risk and a low profit generation.

Routine products are simple products that are attainable everywhere in the world, and the situation calls for simple systems, merely reducing the supplier base world wide. Thus, world-wide coordination is not required because business is local (Van Weele & Rozemeijer). So, the products have both low profit generation and low supplier risk.

This variable is questioned in the 'important location factors' section in the instrument. Instead of using the above category names, the products position in terms of profit generation and supplier risk is used in the related question (e.g. high profit generation/ high supplier risk).

101

Organizational Culture of the Company

Organizational values, beliefs and principles are hard to quantify. Because of this reason, organizational culture of the company is defined by specific management practices and behaviors in the instrument. These practices have a direct effect in decision-making behavior of the company for location factors. Besides, these practices are more quantifiable than abstract practices like values, beliefs and principles. Considering these facts, the variables:

- Involvement: final decision maker in the organization,
- Risk taking: the risk taking behavior of the organization,
- Autonomy: information sharing in the organization and the feedback from managers are questioned in the instrument to determine the management practices of the organization. Only one generic question is asked to extract the major effect of the values, beliefs and principles.

Sector Type

Sector type of the company is questioned in the last section, "Company Information" section of the instrument. Four areas of manufacturing were:

- Fiber
- Textiles
- Apparel
- Nonwovens

Further research might consider more specific areas to have a more in-depth analysis, using this instrument.

External Environment of the Company

External environment of the company encompasses the political issues, economic issues, sociological issues and technological issues. These variables are questioned in the "Important location factors" section of the instrument.

102

Location factors are a set of required criteria used in the location decisions. There are different levels of the location factors: international, regional and site. International level consists of the possible reasons why a particular country might be attractive to an organization. Once the country is selected, more detailed regional location factors appear to consider for the analysis. Afterwards, the in-depth location factors for the organization should be determined for the specific site selection (Schniederjans, 1999). The focus of the instrument is mainly on the international level and specific questions were developed in the instrument to serve this focus.

DISCUSSION

In today's volatile environment, the developed instrument offers distinct advantages for textile and apparel companies. Besides the main purpose of the instrument, which is to create a decision making tool for global investment decisions, specific sections help companies better understand possible changes and be ready for them.

First, "strategic approach of the companies" section can be used as a self-assessment tool for the companies, especially for small and medium size companies. This section ascertains the main objective of the company by questioning its strategic approach and organizational culture. Companies' response to the questions, considering their sector type and the happenings in the external environment, should make them more aware of themselves and their needs. In an interview with an executive from State of North Carolina Department of Commerce, the executive supported the usefulness of the tool. The executive stressed that this instrument would offer great value especially for medium and small sized companies. She mentioned that most of the time, those types of companies were not very well aware of their needs.

Second, after revealing the needs of the company, for global investment decisions, the instrument offers an extensive list of location factors to consider categorized under the following groups:

- ✓ Cost
- ✓ Availability
- ✓ Accessibility
- ✓ Quality
- ✓ Risk/uncertainty
- ✓ Ease of operations
- ✓ Quality of life

Companies can customize the location factors list and rank the factors according to their preferences and consideration of their own needs. In this way, they can generate a specific solution to their problem of locating a global operation.

Researchers, on the other hand, can use this instrument to search the effect of different dimensions like sector type, size of the company, age of the company, etc. on global investment decisions. Results can be analyzed and hopefully more comprehensive and accurate conclusions can be reached.

Organizations like Department of Commerce can use this instrument to offer consequential incentives to the target companies to urge their investment decisions. The executive suggested that research of the decision-making behaviors of companies from different sectors would be very useful for themselves to find out the important location factors for the companies. In this way, she added that they could know which factor to foster/invest as Department of Commerce so that they can offer attractive numbers for those factors. An example could be the decision of allocating budget to education, to infrastructure, to recreational areas, etc. since the significance of these factors would be given accurately using the instrument.

For the textile and apparel industry, the above-mentioned points are even more important than the other industries due to the most global nature of this industry. It is impossible in any other industry to produce each part of the product in different country and manage the sourcing chain of these processes (Birnbaum, 2000). This is especially, with the change in the trade agreements between countries, so that many combinations can be utilized for garment production. Therefore, the accuracy of the decision is so critical for textile and apparel industry.

CONCLUSIONS

Companies invest to grow, to modernize, and to modify their current activities, considering the market dynamics and the frequency of change in the global arena. Traditional investment decision-making process includes three steps: Determine the candidate countries, analyze these countries based on a generic location factors list, and make the final decision. This three-step process, however, embodies serious flaws for today's environment. The process has to be customized for companies' specific needs if they want to outperform their competitors by utilizing the comparative advantages of the countries.

For a meaningful customization, the heart of the process is the second stage where companies analyze countries using an important location factors list. This location factors list, including the importance of the factors, differs based on several dimensions (aspects) of specific companies. Based on the combination of literature review and interviews to obtain the expert opinion from industry, four macro-level dimensions are determined: companies' strategies, their organizational culture, their sector and the external environment in which they operate.

This paper presents a comprehensive instrument for customized investment decisions. This is built upon four main pillars: the strategy of the company, the organizational culture of the company, the sector where the company operates, and the role of external environment. An instrument is developed to guide the companies to an effective customization of the location factors and their priorities according to the

105

companies' needs. The validation of the instrument was conducted using feedback from an expert, who not only emphasized the importance of the instrument but also suggested other ways to use the tool.

As a result, the traditional three-step approach has been modified and an additional step of customization of the location factors is inserted. At this step, companies have to perform a self-assessment process to make accurate and customized decisions using the "Customized Investment Decisions Instrument". This instrument serves as

> ➢ a comprehensive tool since it covers the important dimensions for a company and
> ➢ an effective tool since it provides customization for different needs of the companies.

It is believed that it will be useful if future work can be an implementation of this instrument to different sectors, to model the decision-making behaviors. Another suggestion would be to update the dimensions according to the changing dynamics of the environment. Today the most important and comprehensive dimensions are strategy, culture, sectors type and external environment. However, new dimensions may emerge in the future that should be considered or the definitions of the used dimensions may change and it may be necessary to update the instrument accordingly in the future.

REFERENCES

Andrews, D. C. (1995). Can organizational culture be reengineered? Enterprise Reengineering, Oct/Nov(http://www.c3i.osd.mil/bpr/bprcd/5304.htm).

Bair, J., & Gereffi, G. (2002). NAFTA and the apparel commodity chain:Corporate strategies, interfirm networks, and industrial upgrading. In J. Bair (Ed.), Free Trade and Uneven Development (pp. 356). Philadelphia: Temple University Press.

Birnbaum, D. (2000). Birnbaum's Global Guide to Winning the Great Garment War. Hong Kong: Third Horizon Press Limited.

Brush, T. H., Maritan, C. A., & Karnani, A. (1999). The Plant Location Decision in Multinational Manufacturing Firms:An Emprical Analysis of International Business and Manufacturing Strategy Perspectives. Production and Operations Management, 8(2), 109-132.

Camuffo, A., Romano, P., & Vinelli, A. (2001). Back to the future:Benetton transforms its global network. MIT Sloan Management Review(Fall), 46-52.

Notes on Facility Location. (1989). Harvard Business College

Cox, T. J. (1993). Cultural Diversity in Organizations:Theory, Research & Practice. San Francisco: Berett-Koehler.

Dunning, J. H. (1988). The eclectic paradigm of international production:A restatement and some possible extensions. Journal of International Business Studies(Spring), 1-31.

Hax, A., & Majluf, S. (1983). The Industry Attractiveness-Business Strength Matrix in Strategic Planning. Interfaces, 13(April), 54-71.

Hayter, R. (1997). The Dynamics of Industrial Location:The Factory, The Firm, The Production System. England: John Wiley & Sons.

Henisz, W., & Delios, A. (2001). Uncertainty, Imitation and Plant Location:Japanese multinational corporations, 1990-1996. Administrative Science Quarterly, 46, 443-475.

Higgins, J. M., & Vincze, J. W. (1993). Strategic Management:Text and Cases (Fifth ed.): The Dryden Press.

Hunt, J. R., & Koulamas, C. P. (1989). A Model for Evaluating Potential Facility Locations on a Global Basis. SAM Advanced Management Journal(Summer), 19-23.

Ietto_gillies, G. (2000). What role for Multinationals in the New Theories of International Trade and Location? International Review of Applied Economics, 14(4), 413-426.

MacCarty, B., & Atthirawong, W. (2001). Critical Factors in International Location Decisions: A Delphi study. Paper presented at the Twelfth Annual Conference of the Production and Operations Management Society, Orlando, FL.

Murray, J. Y., & Kotabe, M. (1999). Sourcing strategies of US Service companies: A modified transaction cost analysis. Strategic Management Journal, 20, 791-809.

Porter, M. (1980). Competitive Strategy:Techniques for Analyzing Industries and Competitors: The Free Press.

Porter, M. (1990). The Competitive Advantage of Nations. New York: The Free Press.

Porter, M. (1998). Competing Across Locations:Enhancing Competitive Advantage through Global Strategy: Harvard Business School Press.

Schniederjans, M. J. (1999). International Facility Acquisition and Location Analysis. London: Quorum Books.

Tong, H.-M. (1979). Plant Location Decision of Foreign Manufacturing Investors. Michigan: UMI Research Press.

Ulgado, F. M. (1996). Location Characteristics of Manufacturing Investments in the US: A Comparison of American and Foreign-based Firms. Management International Review, 36(1), 7-24.

Van Weele, A. J., & Rozemeijer, F. A. Revolution in purchasing:Building competitive power through pro-active purchasing. Eindhoven: Technical University.

Verra, G. J. (1999). Global Sourcing : An international survey among multinationals. Paper presented at the Nyenrode Research Papers Series.

PART V: AN EMPIRICAL ANALYSIS OF THE INTERNATIONAL INVESTMENT DECISIONS IN THE US TEXTILE AND APPAREL INDUSTRY

INTRODUCTION

Patterns of global production and trade have changed after several major agreements for the US Textile and Apparel industry. These changes were ignited in 1994 with North American Free Trade Agreement (NAFTA) and exploded with Caribbean Basin Trade Partnership Act (CBTPA), the African Growth and Opportunity Act (AGOA) and other special trade agreements with mostly developing countries. Textile and apparel companies started to exploit their competitive advantages by using the comparative advantage of the different geographical locations.

The first wave of US investments was targeted mainly at Mexico after NAFTA. The leading US textile companies invested millions of dollars in operations like spinning, dyeing and finishing, and sewing to strengthen their positions in the North American region. Since the first wave of investments, attention has shifted to various parts of the world like the Caribbean, Asia, and South Africa. However, not every one of these decisions was successful for the investors.

Unexpectedly, several leading textile companies i.e., Burlington Industries and Guilford Mills, both of Greensboro, NC announced Chapter 11 within the last five years[22]. Perhaps, the failure of these types of international investment decisions has very much contributed to the struggle of the US textile and apparel companies. Newspapers have published articles, which discussed the failure of the leading textile companies in Mexico. One of the comments was in the News & Record, "On an otherwise empty plot of land in eastern Mexico sits what some are calling Guilford Mills' $40 million failure." (Heisler, 2003). Although failures were experienced when investments were made outside of the home country, it is also clear that staying in one's home country is not automatically the right decision for all types of the textile companies. Some companies only focused on the generic objective of lowering costs without even considering if this objective

---

[22] http://www.textileweb.com/

supported their internal needs. Others considered some countries without examining the macro-level performance of the countries like country culture. The country may propose a lot of advantages; however, these advantages may not offer a competitive advantage to the company.

The purpose of this paper is to understand the decision-making process of the textile and apparel companies for international investment decisions. The effect of internal environment of a company was analyzed on the international investment decisions using a survey and a case study research methodology. Three research objectives are identified:

RO1: To determine the effect of strategy on location factors

- Corporate strategy

- Specific operational strategy

- Product strategy

- Growth strategy

RO2: To determine the effect of organizational culture on location factors

RO3: To determine the effect of the sector type on location factors

LITERATURE REVIEW

Empirical studies for investment decisions have started in 1970s. However, it was limited to the plant locations in the US until the 1980s. An in-depth review of literature related to this section is available and discussed in Parts III and IV.

METHODOLOGY

Research Design

An exploratory survey research methodology was chosen to collect data on international investment decisions. However, after starting the data collection, the survey method appeared to be ineffective due to the sensitive subject matter that was asked in the survey. Most of the companies either rejected or did not answer the e-mail request since strategic and proprietary information about their companies were asked. Reasons for rejections are discussed in detail in the following section. Thus, a new research methodology was selected (Figure 16). Survey methodology was used to acquire descriptive data on important location factors for textile and apparel companies. Case study methodology was conducted to enhance the results of the survey and to obtain in-depth data for international investment decisions. So, with this methodology, the unexpected consequences of using a survey method are overcome. In addition, the richness of data is increased since companies shared their investment experiences in detail.

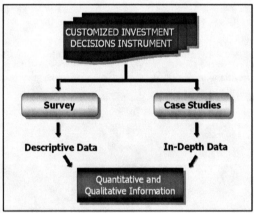

Figure 16 Research methodology

Instrument Development

Customized Investment Decisions Instrument[23] was used for both survey implementation and case studies. A field test was conducted with an executive from a leading apparel company to validate the relevance of the instrument for the study.

Sample Selection

The sample of 75 companies was selected from the following data sources (Table 14):

Table 14 Data sources for sample selection

ASSOCIATIONS	DATA SOURCES
Partners of Nonwoven Cooperative Research Center (NCRC), NCSU	http://www.tx.ncsu.edu/ncrc/Member%20Companies.html
American Fiber Manufacturers Association Inc.	http://www.fibersource.com/afma/members.htm
Knitted Textile Association	http://www.kta-usa.org/
The Hosiery Association	http://www.nahm.com/hsymem/alphalist.asp
American Yarn Spinners Association	www.aysa.org
American Textile Manufacturers Institute	http://www.atmi.org/Pubs/alltexother.asp
INFORMATION SOURCES	
Corporate Affiliations- business information source	www.corporateaffiliations.com
James Girone's online guide to children's fashion	http://jamesgirone.com/manufacturers/manufacturers_s.htm
Hoover's - business information source	www.hoovers.com
U.S. Supima Licensees	http://www.supimacotton.org/supima/licUs.htm
JOURNALS	
Textile Industries Media Group	www.textileindustries.com
Home Textiles Today	NCSU Library Database
Textile Outlook International	NCSU Library

Using the above sources, companies were selected based on a set of selection criteria, listed below.

1. Sector:

---

[23] This instrument is discussed at Part IV.

- o Fiber (SIC 28)

- o Textiles (SIC 2211, 2281, 2282)

- o Apparel (SIC 23)

- o Nonwoven (SIC 2297)

2. Top companies operating in the above sectors are selected using data sources. Additional companies were considered based on the faculty recommendation.

3. Companies should embody at least one of the following experiences:

- o An international plant outside of the states

- o Any kind of strategic alliances with a plant outside of the US

- o No plants outside of the US however, experience of considering global investments

Contact information was found using the lists in the above data sources, company web sites, and the using university personnel in their contacts.

Data Collection

The instrument was posted on the Internet[24] using an online form. Data was written to a Microsoft Excel® file. A four-step data collection strategy, which was a modified version of Don A. Dilmann's guidelines[25], was used. First contact was performed with a pre-notification letter (Appendix C-1) which was sent to the generic e-mail addresses, found on the websites of the related companies. The second contact was a cover letter with the online survey link (Appendix C-2). After the second step, some responses were received from companies about the difficulties in opening the survey website due to company firewalls. Therefore, the online implementation plan was changed because of the technical difficulties and the below-than-expected response rate.

---

[24] The URL for the online survey is http://www4.ncsu.edu/~suncu/survey/
[25] See Dillmann (2000) for details.

A copy of the survey was then faxed to the companies that experienced difficulties in opening the survey website.

A week after the second contact, a thank you card (Appendix C-3) was sent to the companies. This letter was a thank-you message for the companies who already responded the survey and a reminder message for the others who had not sent any response yet. The fourth and final contact was the last request for filling out the survey (Appendix C-4). Besides e-mail, telephone contacts were conducted as a final contact to increase the below-than-expected response rate.

There occurred a four-week time gap between the third and the final contact. This was due to the adjustment in the research design explained in the above section. The acceptance and rejection rates of the survey are illustrated in Table 15 for each step.

Table 15 Acceptance and rejection rates

	First Contact	Second Contact	Third Contact	Fourth Contact	Total
Rejection	5	10	0	3	13
Acceptance	0	7	1	9	17
Total Responses					30

Case study methodology was decided and a convenience sample of companies was selected. Case study request was sent out via e-mail for five of the six companies. For one leading textiles company, the executive contacted the author requesting a discussion about the research topic in person. He specifically mentioned that he was in the process of making international investment decisions. The rest of the case studies were also conducted in person. Two of the six companies have filled out the survey prior to in person case studies. Their responses were discussed in detail during the interviews. For three of them, first a general discussion about their past international investment

115

decisions was conducted and then the survey was filled out. The reason to conduct the general discussion first was due to the aim of preventing the bias for their responses.

Response Rate and Usable Sample Size

The companies, who declined participation, were eliminated after each step. A total of 55 companies did not reply to any of the contacts. Rejection reasons are stated in Table 16.

Table 16 Reasons for rejection

Reasons for Rejection	Number of companies
"Much of what you ask for in the way of information and strategies is considered proprietary and could not be shared in a study of this type."	2
"Due to the sheer volume of requests of this kind, we are unable to provide detailed information", "we do not have time"	3
Decline to participate with no reason	8

The removal of these companies from the original sample resulted in a final sample size of 17, and a 23% response rate (n=75) was achieved (Table 17). This response rate is higher than the average response rate (21%) of the industry surveys (Dillman, 2000).

Table 17 Useable sample size per sector

	Surveys Sent	Usable Returned Surveys	Response Rate (%)
Fiber	11	2	18
Textile	41	8	20
Apparel	13	6	46
Nonwoven	10	1	10
TOTAL	**75**	**17**	**23**

Data Analysis

All of the electronic and paper responses were collected into a Microsoft Excel® file. The responses are coded according to the codebook developed for the "Customized Investment Decisions Instrument". Due to the limited number of the usable surveys, descriptive statistics are used. The descriptive statistics is applied to data set were:

➢ Mean

➢ Median and Mode

➢ Range, Minimum and Maximum

➢ Sum and Count

Case studies are then used to enhance the survey results. Since 5 of the 6 case study companies filled out the survey, the case studies provide a better understanding of the results.

RESULTS

Sample Description

The research sample for survey implementation comprised 17 companies from fiber, textile, apparel and nonwovens sectors. To support and lend a greater understanding of the limited survey results, case studies were conducted with 5 of these 17 companies and with a fiber company outside the survey research sample. The reason to select this outside company was to support the limited data that was collected with the survey method. The same effort was spent to find a company to support the nonwovens area, but none of the companies contacted were available for participation.

Detailed information about the survey respondents is shown in Table 18. Company name, location of the company, sector type, number of employees (2001-

117

2002), total sales (2001-2002) are presented to provide the characteristics of the survey sample[26]. Company names are masked and intervals are used to present the number of employees and total sales data to ensure the confidentiality of the participated companies.

Table 18 Sample description

Company Name	Location	Sector Type	Employees	Sales (million $)	Business Ranking 2001-2002
A	North Carolina	Fiber	4001-4500	750-1000	12[1]
B	North Carolina	Textiles	3001-3500	250-500	10[2]
C	South Carolina	Textiles	15001-20000	2000-2500	2[2]
D	Georgia	Textiles	1-500	250-500	N/A
E	North Carolina	Textiles	2501-3000	750-1000	1[2]
F	North Carolina	Textiles	501-1000	100-250	N/A
G	North Carolina	Textiles	4001-4500	500-750	2[2]
H	North Carolina	Textiles	2001-2500	500-750	45[2]
I	North Carolina	Textiles	5501-6000	500-750	1[2]
J	North Carolina	Textiles	25001-30000	100-250	4[2]
K	North Carolina	Apparel	over 55000	5000-5250	1[1]
L	North Carolina	Apparel	1-500	500-750	1[1]
M	Missouri	Apparel	25001-30000	2000-2500	1[2]
N	Wisconsin	Apparel	2001-2500	500-750	N/A
O	Georgia	Apparel	10000-15000	1000-1250	1[2]
P	Oregon	Apparel	20000-25000	9500-9750	N/A
R	North Carolina	Nonwoven	501-1000	1250-1500	1[3]

[1]Business rankings were taken from Dun & Bradstreet Business Rankings 2001
[2]Business rankings were taken from Ward's Business Directory 2002.
For N/A, Ranking is not available with secondary data sources. SIC is not given in order to ensure company confidentiality.
[3]Business rankings were taken from World Market Share Reporter 2001-2002.

---

[26] Source of these data is the Hoovers' website: http://www.hoovers.com

118

Sample description for the case studies is presented in Table 19. Since 5 of the 6 companies filled out the survey, the same company labels are used to present these companies. The last company, which was not in the survey sample, is named as Company S.

Table 19 Sample description for case studies

Company Name	Interviewee	Sector Type
A	• Global Analysis Manager • Global Market Analyst	Fiber and Textile
D	• CEO	Textile
E	• Former President	Textile
O	• Executive Vice President • Vice President, Supply Chain	Apparel
R	• General Manager	Nonwovens
S	• Former Plant Manager • Accounts Manager (Europe, Middle East & Africa)	Fiber

Company/Respondent Information

The breakdown of the 17 responses based on the sector type is stated in Table 20. Four of the seventeen companies put themselves in more than one sector. Therefore, their responses were tallied considering the sector where majority of business is conducted.

The majority (53%, n=17) of the respondents were from textile companies. These companies include yarn, fabric, and home textiles manufacturers. Companies in this section include the top companies in terms of sales data (see the business rankings column in Table 18). The second largest category is the apparel manufacturers (35%, n=17). Four of the 6 companies are ranked as first in the related SIC categories based on the sales data. Information was not available for the other two companies. The representation for the fiber and nonwoven companies were very limited. However, they are both leading fiber and nonwoven producers.

Table 20 Respondent percentages by sector type

Sector	Percentage (n=17)
Fiber	6%
Textiles	53%
Apparel	35%
Nonwoven	6%

In terms of international investments, nearly every company (88%, n=17) has an international operation (either manufacturing or strategic partners). The fiber company and the nonwoven company are global companies with manufacturing facilities in Americas, Europe, and Asia. Most of the textile companies (77%) have international investments in Mexico, Caribbean and Latin America. Some of them (33%) also have manufacturing facilities and strategic partners in Europe. All of the apparel companies have international investment experience of Americas, Caribbean, Asia, and Europe.

More than half of the respondents have been with their company for more than 10 years and sixteen out of seventeen of the respondents are part of the final decision making process.

Nine of the 17 companies use customer/market research and scenario analysis as a tool to determine locations for new greenfield operations. Two of them use decision trees and other two companies use simulation for the same type of decision-making.

Results

Responses were analyzed according to the research objectives of the study. The main objective is to determine the effects of different dimensions[27] on location factors. Therefore, each section starts with the introduction of the dimension, which is questioned in the research objective and continues with the ratings of the location

---

[27] See Part IV for the explanation of dimension and variable.

factors that are grouped under seven categories[28]: cost, availability, accessibility, quality, risk/uncertainty, ease of operations, and quality of life. The rankings were arranged according to the related variables of each dimension where applicable, mean values were compared for most of the case studies. Descriptive statistical results of the rankings by the different variables are stated in Appendix D-I. The mean scores of each variable is depicted using a radar (spider) chart[29]. This graphical representation is selected because one can easily see the overall inclination of the sample and the specific values of the variables and their difference from the maximum and the minimum value in one chart. In this chart, the value increases from the center to the outer layers of the chart. The value differs from 0 to 4 since this scale was used to rank the variables in the survey (1 = UNIMPORTANT, 2 = LESS IMPORTANT, 3 = IMPORTANT, 4 = VERY IMPORTANT). The number of the corners of the chart is equal to the number of the variables in a group. In other words, the corners of the chart represent the variables.

At the end of each section for variables of the research objectives, a summary table was created based on the survey and case study results if there are significant differences among the ratings of the variables. Three sections are formed in the tables considering the importance level of the factors:

- Must Factors,
- Highly recommended factors
- Optional factors

---

[28] See Part IV for detailed information about categories.

[29] Microsoft Office® Assistance Center

121

Research Objective 1: To determine the effect of strategy on location factors

Strategy dimension is defined with four variables in "Customized Investment Decisions Instrument". They are corporate strategy, growth strategy, operational strategy and product strategy. These strategies are further divided into sub-variables and ratings of the location factors are analyzed based on these sub-variables.

Variable I: Corporate Strategy

Corporate strategy is defined with three sub-variables: cost leadership, differentiation and focus(niche)[30]. Forty one-percent of the *survey respondents* (n=17) chose differentiation, thirty five-percent chose cost leadership and the rest chose focus as their corporate strategy.

None of the fiber and nonwoven companies stated cost leadership as their corporate strategy. The majority (55%, n=9) of those who chose cost leadership were from textile companies. Seventeen-percent of the apparel companies (n=6) chose cost leadership as their corporate strategy.

The fiber (100%, n=1) company indicated that differentiation was its corporate strategy. Majority of the apparel companies (83%, n=6) stated differentiation as their corporate strategy. In textile companies (n=9), this percentage dropped to 11%.

---

[30] See Part IV

Focus (niche) strategy was chosen by 33% of the textiles companies. The nonwoven company (100%, n=1) also selected this strategy as its corporate strategy. None of the apparel companies chose focus (niche) strategy.

Case study interviewees were evenly distributed among the sub-variables. Out of six companies, two of them selected differentiation, two of them selected cost leadership and the rest selected focus as their corporate strategy. A summary of the survey and case study responses for corporate strategy is stated in Table 21.

Table 21 The distribution of the survey and case study results for corporate strategy

	Cost Leadership	Differentiation	Focus	TOTAL
Survey Results	6	7	4	**17**
Case Study Results	2	2	2	**6**

Location factors

Location rankings are arranged according to the cost leadership, differentiation, and focus sub-variables. Seven groups of location factors are discussed in the following section.

COST

Survey Results

There were no apparent differences in most of the factors under the cost category (Figure 17). 'Total cost of the product' was reported to be VERY IMPORTANT for all companies. However, it was slightly less important for focus companies than the rest. This difference is expected since focus (niche) strategists' first priority is not the 'total cost of the product'. Their primary focus is either the market (niche markets) or the product (niche products) and the design and development of these aspects. When they succeed in these aspects, they can require high profit margins for their products. These

123

high profits margins may cause them to choose 'total cost of product' as slightly a less important factor compared to other strategists.

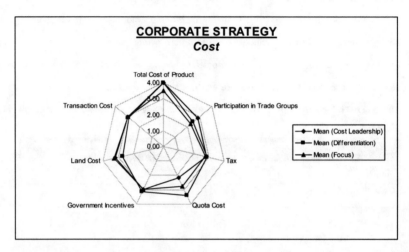

Figure 17 Mean comparisons of the location factors under cost category according to the corporate strategy

There were no apparent differences in most of the factors under the cost category (Figure 17). 'Total cost of the product' was reported to be VERY IMPORTANT for all companies. However, it was slightly less important for focus companies than the rest. This difference is expected since focus (niche) strategists' first priority is not the 'total cost of the product'. Their primary concern is either the market (niche markets) or the product (niche products) and the design and development of these aspects. When they succeed in these aspects, they can require high profit margins for their products. These high profits margins may cause them to choose 'total cost of product' as slightly a less important factor compared to other strategists.

Interestingly, quota cost was rated differently among the strategist. One can expect that this factor should be the most important for the cost leadership followers.

However, it was more important for differentiation strategists than for the others. One reason might be the sector type influence on this variable. Although every variable was considered as independent for the study, one can realize the effect of sector type in this situation. Since the differentiation group encompasses mostly the apparel manufacturers, their product may require more attention for quota costs due to massive amount of sourcing from all around the world.

<u>Case Study Results</u>

All of the companies (n=6) agreed on the importance of the 'total cost of product' factor. In addition to this factor, cost leadership strategists (33%, n=6) stressed the importance of the specific components of this factor like energy costs, labor costs and any training rebates for labor.

One differentiator company mentioned that two of their MOST IMPORTANT reasons for moving to a Latin American location, were "to overcome the high tariff barriers" and "to take the advantage of the low raw material cost". Since the company is a differentiation strategist, it was not expected that these factors would appear to be the most important two reasons. However, the interviewee mentioned that these factors are considered at the very last stage of the decision-making process. This may be explained by assuming that the effect of differentiation strategy (corporate strategy) appears at the beginning of the country selection process. When the candidate countries list is reduced down to a couple of countries, other dimensions may have a higher impact on the location factors.

As a support to the different stages in the decision-making process, two interviewees (Company R and Company S) mentioned that 'government incentives' gains importance at the very last stage (site selection) of the decision-making.

AVAILABILITY

125

In Figure 18, 'availability of transportation' and 'infrastructure' were selected as the MOST IMPORTANT factors for each strategy group. However, there were noticeable differences in how respondents ranked the 'availability of skilled labor' and 'new markets' factors.

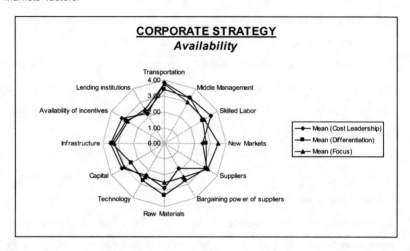

Figure 18 Mean comparisons of the location factors under availability category according to the corporate strategy

Skilled labor was ranked an IMPORTANT factor overall, but, cost leadership strategists considered the 'availability of skilled labor' factor more important than the other strategists. They considered the training and turnover rate of the employees as an additional cost to the 'total cost of product'. So, the reason of that difference may be because of the cost leaders' need to reduce these additional costs.

Focus strategists, on the other hand, considered availability of new markets as a VERY IMPORTANT factor. For US companies, international locations mean a place to produce only; typically, they have not considered marketing their products internationally. For niche/ focus producers, finding new niche markets or new markets for their niche products is a part of their strategy. Therefore, this factor has a considerable importance for focus strategists. The rankings of other factors can be seen in Figure 18.

Case Study Results

One of the two cost leadership strategists stressed the importance of 'availability of raw material and suppliers', and 'availability of skilled labor', which supports the findings of the survey results. One of the two focus strategists also mentioned that 'availability of skilled labor' was an important factor for them.

In addition, both of the differentiators mentioned that this factor was very important for them. "Most of the time we know where the market is going. The gap between the supply and demand plus the per capita consumption are the evidences of the change in the market dynamics," said the executive of one of the differentiator strategists. These results support the survey results about this location factor.

Focus strategists (n=2) mentioned the importance of markets. However, both of the companies made their move after capturing a market share in one location. They first sent their marketing team to the location and when they reached a reasonable market share, and then they decided to locate a plant in that country. This result conflicts with the survey results. There may be the effect of organizational culture in these two instances. Risk taking level of the companies might be low due to the high amount of investment for greenfield operations.

ACCESSIBILITY

Survey Results

Nearly all of the factors in this category were ranked as IMPORTANT for each sub-variable (Figure 19). There are differences in the 'flexibility of production', 'proximity to markets' and 'demographics of industry' factors. Demographics appeared to be the least important factor for cost leaders. There is a dilemma with this factor since the same companies considered 'proximity to suppliers', which is a demographic factor, as

127

IMPORTANT as other strategists. Implicitly, 'proximity to suppliers' factor embodies the demographics of the industry from suppliers' side of the supply chain. If the 'proximity to suppliers' is IMPORTANT for every company, it was expected that cost leaders rated this factor higher than the rest of the strategists.

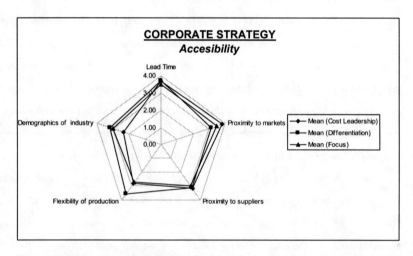

Figure 19 Mean comparisons of the location factors under accessibility category according to the corporate strategy

There is also a difference in the 'flexibility of production'[31] factor. Differentiators gave more importance to this factor than the other strategists. One way of creating differentiation is to differentiate the product line. Companies who follow this strategy may want to produce more than one product in the selected location and may force manufacturers to be flexible within the similar product category to serve their corporate strategy.

---

[31] Flexibility of production refers to the ability of being flexible in the similar product category

Case Study Results

Differentiation strategists stressed, particularly, the importance of 'proximity to markets/customers' factor in this category. In addition, one of the cost leaders mentioned that this factor was the fundamental belief of their company. However, the effect of sector type is clear in this factor. Companies who are at the beginning of the supply chain (fiber and textile companies) follow their customers since most of the apparel companies are either sourcing or forming strategic partnerships with companies all around the world.

On the other hand, both of the focus strategists made a plant location decision to be able to get closer to their customers/markets. Thus, 'proximity to markets' was the main objective for their plant location decisions. This result supports the survey results. Once again, focus strategists aggressively follow their customers since the market that they serve, most of the time, is relatively dense and small.

QUALITY

Regardless of the corporate strategy, all of the factors in this category were VERY IMPORTANT for companies (Figure 20). These results were the same for the case studies. All of them mentioned the importance of the factors in this category. One of the executives said, "These factors are given today. We do not do business with the companies who cannot fully accomplish these requirements".

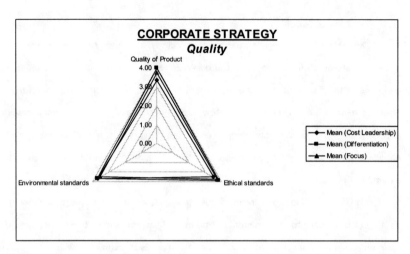

Figure 20 Mean comparisons of the location factors under quality category according to the corporate strategy

RISK/UNCERTAINTY

<u>Survey Results</u>

In Figure 21, delivery reliability and political stability were the most important factors in this category for each group. 'Labor unions' factor was also critical for all of them. It was more critical for cost leaders since labor unions could directly affect labor costs.

There is a difference in the ranking of 'location of the competitors' factor. Focus strategists considered this factor in the upper quartile of the importance scale. Most of the time focus strategists have a handful of competitors and it may be more important for focus strategists to follow what their competitors are doing.

'National content laws of the countries' factor appeared to be more important for cost leaders and focus strategists than the differentiators. The effect of sector type may be seen in this result. Mostly apparel companies are the differentiators in the survey

130

sample.   This factor, however, is more critical for fiber and textile companies since content laws about different chemicals and additives are critical at the fabric manufacturing level.   Apparel companies use these fabrics for their products and they can choose their suppliers accordingly if the national content law prohibits usage of some kind of a material. This difference in the nature of the business (sector type) might be the reason for the difference in the ranking of 'national content laws of the countries' factor.

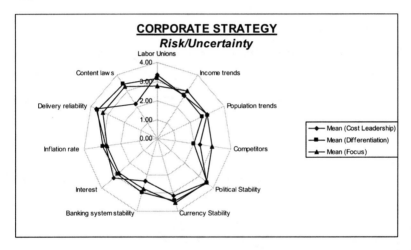

Figure 21 Mean comparisons of the location factors under risk/uncertainty category according to the corporate strategy

<u>Case Study Results</u>

During the cases studies, executives mostly emphasized the political instability in specific countries and the consequences locating in one particular country over another. Some of them implicitly mentioned the importance of delivery reliability by explaining the risks of hijackers, pirates. One company mentioned the risk of the imitation of their proprietary knowledge, which is inevitable with technology transfer when locating to less developed countries.   This factor can be added to the list as the 'country culture'. One executive suggested the ability to get money out of the company as an additional factor to the list, besides banking system stability.

Factors like 'income trends' and 'population trends' are useful for some companies to predict the future. One executive mentioned that they attempt to predict the market by analyzing these trends.

EASE OF OPERATIONS

Survey Results

Export and import rules and taxation of foreign owned companies were the most important factors for all of the strategy groups (Figure 22). However, there was an apparent difference in 'participation in economic trade groups' factor. Cost leaders considered this factor as an IMPORTANT factor, whereas other strategists ranked this factor as LESS IMPORTANT.

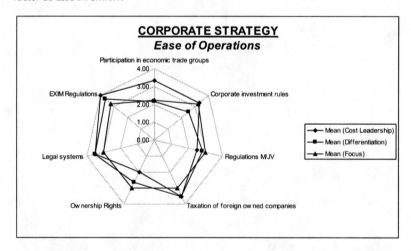

Figure 22 Mean comparisons of the location factors under ease of operations category according to the corporate strategy

For differentiators and focus (niche) strategists, the decision of where to produce is, theoretically, not as cost driven. They decide where to produce based on the product type or market. However for cost leaders, specific regulations among countries are important since these regulations help them quantify their costs (e.g., tax, quota costs). Other results can clearly be seen in Figure 22.

Case Study Results

One of the cost leaders in the case study sample mentioned trade legislations as one of the most important factor from its three-factor list of low cost, training rebates and trade legislations. This comment supports the above survey results.

QUALITY OF LIFE

Survey Results

'Per capita income' was clearly a MORE IMPORTANT factor for differentiators and focus group than the cost leaders (Figure 23). This difference occurred since differentiators and focus strategists consider a new location as a new opportunity to market the product more than a cost leader. So, the buying power of the people is important for them. For cost leaders, a new place means just another place to produce. For all of the strategists, cost of living appeared to be an important factor in this category with temperature rating the least.

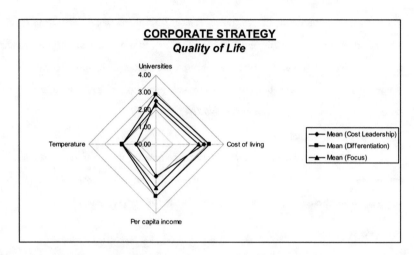

Figure 23 Mean comparisons of the location factors under quality of life category according to the corporate strategy

Case Study Results

In case studies, there was no major emphasis on this group of factors.

Summary of the Results for Variable I: Corporate Strategy

Table 22 is the summary table for corporate strategy. Three variables (cost leadership, differentiation and focus) are put in each column in the table and factor groups are placed in the rows. Three sections (must, highly recommended and optional) are divided by dotted lines.

Table 22 Summary table for corporate strategy

		Cost Leadership	Differentiation	Focus
Cost	*Must*	Total Cost of Product Transaction Costs Government Incentives Tax Land Cost	Total Cost of Product Transaction Costs Government Incentives Tax Quota Cost Land Cost	Total Cost of Product Transaction Costs Government Incentives Tax Land Cost Quota Cost
	Highly recommended	Participation in economic trade groups	Participation in economic trade groups	Participation in economic trade groups
	Optional	Quota Cost		
Availability	*Must*	Availability of transportation Availability of infrastructure Availability of suppliers Availability of middle management Availability of skilled labor	Availability of transportation Availability of infrastructure Availability of suppliers Availability of middle management Availability of raw materials	Availability of transportation Availability of infrastructure Availability of suppliers Availability of middle management Availability of new markets
	Highly recommended	Availability of raw materials Availability of capital Availability of incentives Availability of new markets	Bargaining power of suppliers Availability of incentives Availability of new markets Availability of skilled labor	Availability of raw materials Bargaining power of suppliers Availability of capital Availability of incentives Availability of skilled labor
	Optional	Bargaining power of suppliers Availability of technology Availability of lending institutions	Availability of capital Availability of technology Availability of lending institutions	Availability of technology Availability of lending institutions
Accessibility	*Must*	Lead Time Proximity to markets Proximity to suppliers	Lead Time Proximity to markets Proximity to suppliers Flexibility of production Demographics of industry	Lead Time Proximity to markets Proximity to suppliers Demographics of industry
	Highly recommended	Flexibility of production Demographics of industry		Flexibility of production
	Optional			
Quality	*Must*	Quality of Product Environmental standards Ethical standards	Quality of Product Environmental standards Ethical standards	Quality of Product Environmental standards Ethical standards

Table 22 (con't)

		Cost Leadership	Differentiation	Focus
Risk/Uncertainty	*Must*	Delivery Reliability Political Stability Currency Stability Inflation Rate Labor Unions Income Trends Population trends Interest Rate National content laws of the country	Delivery Reliability Political Stability Currency Stability Inflation Rate Banking system stability Labor Unions Income Trends Population trends Interest Rate	Delivery Reliability Political Stability Currency Stability Inflation Rate Location of the competitors Banking system stability Income Trends Population trends Interest Rate National content laws of the country
	Highly recommended	Location of the competitors Banking system stability		Labor Unions
	Optional		Location of the competitors National content laws of the country	
Ease of operations	*Must*	Participation in economic trade groups Corporate investment rules Taxation of foreign owned companies Legal systems Export/Import Regulations	Regulations MJV Taxation of foreign owned companies Ownership rights Legal systems Export/Import Regulations	Corporate investment rules Regulations MJV Taxation of foreign owned companies Ownership rights Legal systems Export/Import Regulations
	Highly recommended	Regulations MJV	Participation in economic trade groups Corporate investment rules	Participation in economic trade groups
	Optional	Ownership rights		
Quality of Life	*Must*	Cost of living	Cost of living Per capita income Availability of universities, colleges	Per capita income
	Highly recommended	Availability of universities, colleges		Availability of universities, colleges
	Optional	Per capita income Temperature	Temperature	Cost of living Temperature

136

Variable II: Growth Strategy

Growth strategy is defined with three sub-variables: greenfield operations, strategic partnership and sourcing[32]. The question asked was, "How important are each one of the following types of international investments for your company?". Companies were asked to rank the importance levels of these strategies. The scale was from 1 to 4, 1 being UNIMPORTANT and 4 being VERY IMPORTANT. The sub-variable means are calculated according to the responses of the companies. Only the values of '3' (IMPORTANT) and '4' (VERY IMPORTANT) were taken into consideration in determining the means. For example, if a company ranked greenfield operation as VERY IMPORTANT (4), then this company's location factor ratings were considered under the greenfield operations variable. Table 23 shows the distribution of the responses. Although the question asked respondents to rank the importance of the choice, they also let them select more than one option. This selection allows for more than the total number of the respondents for each variable.

Table 23 The distribution of the survey and case study results for growth strategy

	Greenfield Operations	Strategic Partnerships	Sourcing
Survey Results	9	11	13
Case Study Results	4	5	3

Fiber company (n=1) ranked every sub-variable as IMPORTANT. Textile companies (n=10) ranked strategic partnerships as the most important growth strategy among other strategies. Greenfield operations and sourcing are still important for these companies but their importance appears less than the strategic partnership strategy.

For apparel companies (n=6) greenfield operations strategy were LESS IMPORTANT. They ranked sourcing as the most important strategy, followed by the strategic

---

[32] See Part IV

partnerships strategy. Nonwoven companies (n=1) selected strategic partnerships strategy as VERY IMPORTANT. Sourcing is IMPORTANT for them, however, they consider greenfield operations UNIMPORTANT. This result contradicts with the case study results. A case study was conducted with the company and their priorities discussed after conducting a greenfield operation.

Given the above distributions, each group (cost, availability, accessibility, quality, risk/uncertainty, ease of operations and quality of life) in the important location factors list was analyzed considering these three variables. No distinct prioritization was found in the rankings of the importance levels of the factors among different growth strategies.

From the case studies, one of the greenfield operation selector mentioned the importance of 'government incentives'. This is understandable since governments provide a wide range of incentives when a company decides to invest millions of dollars in one of their locations. The other greenfield operations selector mentioned the importance of factors that are really important after the investment. The factors were the 'availability of skilled labor', 'suppliers', and 'raw materials'. On the other hand one of the sourcing selectors emphasized the importance of trade legislations. This is logical when the vast amount of trade and specific privileges with the trade legislations are concerned for the sourcing companies.

In conclusion, case study results compensated for the insufficient data collected by the survey implementation. Still, there were not so many differences among variables; however, some meaningful conclusions were derived from the case studies. This conclusion also proves the accuracy of selecting case study strategy to enhance the survey results.

Variable III: Operational Strategy

Operational strategy is defined with five variables: innovation, quality, continuous improvement, speed, flexibility, and other[33]. The question asked was, "Which of the following/s describes your company's specific practices? (Select all that apply)." Seventy-six percent of the respondents selected 'innovation' as a specific operational practice that they follow. 'Quality' was selected by 95% of the respondents. Seventy-one percent of them selected both 'continuous improvement' and 'innovation' as their operational practices, and 'flexibility' was selected by seventy-six percent.

Over seventy percent of the sample selected all of the specific practices as important. Case studies supported the survey results. Most of the companies selected at least three of the five operational strategies. Therefore, there are no differences among the variables, and the charts are more or less the same with the overall response charts. Thus, it is concluded that operational strategies, by themselves, do not appear to have any impact on how they ranked the factors for international investment decisions.

Variable IV: Product Strategy

Product strategy is defined with four sub-variables: products with

- high profit, but high risk
- high profit , and low risk
- low profit and low risk
- low profit, but high risk

These variables were defined in detail in Part IV. One-third of the companies (30%, n=17) of the surveyed companies mentioned that they ranked the importance of the location factors considering their high profit generator, but high supplier risk products. Slightly more than one-third of the companies (35%, n=17) selected high profit generator and low supplier risk products. Low profit generator and low risk

---

[33] See Part IV

139

products were the choice of one-third of the companies (30%, n=17). Only one company (5%, n=17) selected low profit but high-risk products. The distribution of survey results and case study results are stated in Table 24.

Table 24 The distribution of the survey and case study results for product strategy

	High profit / High risk	High profit / Low risk	Low profit / low risk	Low profit / high risk	TOTAL
Survey Results	5	6	5	1	17
Case Study Results	2	2	2	-	6

Location factors

COST

Survey Results

'Total cost of product' was VERY IMPORTANT for all of the companies (Figure 24). 'Participation in economic trading group' factor was IMPORTANT for every group but "low profit/low risk" group. One reason for this difference might be the low supplier risk of the product. If there is plethora of suppliers available outside, they may not chase the specific countries with trade agreements. This reason should also be applicable to the other low risk group (high profit/low risk).

However, this is not the case. Since the difference of the other low risk group is that it generates high profit from the products, it can still chase specific advantages to increase their profit margin. That might be the reason for 'high profit/low risk' group to rank the factor as IMPORTANT.

'Low Profit' groups gave most of the cost factors more importance than the 'high profit' groups. Since the profit margins of the first group are low, they may consider the cost factors more seriously than the other groups.

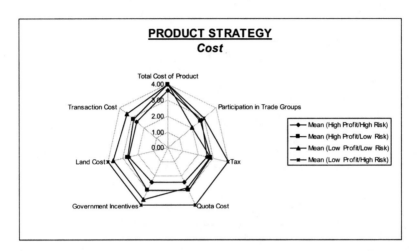

Figure 24 Mean comparisons of the location factors under cost category according to the product strategy

<u>Case Study Results</u>

All of the companies mentioned the importance of 'total cost of product'. The low profit / low risk group highlighted the importance of cost factors. On the contrary to the survey results, one of the low profit/low risk companies mentioned that 'participation in economic trade groups' of the country was critical for them.

AVAILABILITY

<u>Survey Results</u>

As expected, the groups with high supplier risk ranked 'availability of suppliers' factors higher than the other groups (Figure 25). However, the same result was expected in 'bargaining power of suppliers' factor. The high profit/high risk group ranked it as LESS IMPORTANT. Since this factor affects the price of the product, they may not be as conscious as the low profit group.

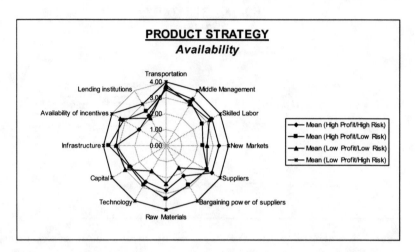

Figure 25 Mean comparisons of the location factors under availability category according to the product strategy

Differences in the other factors can be due to the effects of other variables (e.g., sector type, corporate strategy) on the ranking. There are no significant explanations when product strategy is considered for these variables.

Case Study Results

In case studies, high profit group ranked the availability of new markets as VERY IMPORTANT. Most of the companies (75%, n=4) locate plants or form strategic alliances, if new markets are available in the country. This result somewhat contradicts with the survey result since high profit/low risk companies ranked 'availability of new markets as LESS IMPORTANT. In this case, the effect of other variables would be revealed in the survey results since the case study results seem logical. High profit products usually are the specialty or niche products. Companies can demand a higher price for those types of products since they are unique or rare in the market. However, the potential size of the

142

market of these types of products is limited. Thus, it is logical for high profit group to chase the new markets.

ACCESSIBILITY

<u>Survey Results</u>

There was an apparent difference in 'flexibility of production' factor (Figure 26). The 'low profit/low risk' group ranked this factor as LESS IMPORTANT. Most of the time products in this group are commodity products. They may not require a high flexibility in the production.

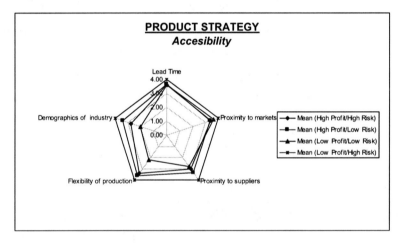

Figure 26 Mean comparisons of the location factors under accessibility category according to the product strategy

<u>Case Study Results</u>

'Proximity to markets' factor is selected by all of the companies in high profit/low risk and high profit/ high risk groups and by one company in low profit/low risk group. The other company in that category is already near to its customer/markets. Thus, this might be the reason for the company not concentrating on this factor. In general,

143

companies, regardless of their product type, are very concerned about being close to their markets/customers.

QUALITY

Factors in the 'quality' group are ranked as very important for every group in the survey and in the case studies for product strategy.

RISK/UNCERTAINTY

Survey Results

They all rated political stability, inflation rate, currency stability, and delivery reliability as IMPORTANT (Figure 27). 'Location of competitors' factor had differences among product strategists. The ones with high risk ranked this factor as more important than the others. Since they have high risks (uncertainty), they may want to know their competitors' relationships with the suppliers.

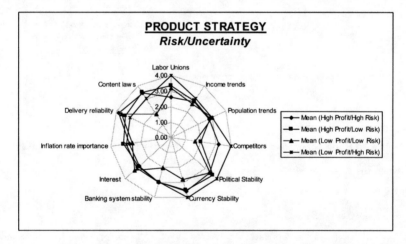

Figure 27 Mean comparisons of the location factors under risk/uncertainty category according to the product strategy

144

'National content laws of the country' factor ranked as LESS IMPORTANT by low profit/low risk group. This difference cannot be explained by product strategy. There may be the effects of the other variables in this factor. Other marginal differences cannot happen because of the product strategy either.

Case Study Results

There was not any important comment on the sub-variables in this category during case study interviews.

EASE OF OPERATIONS

There are no significant differences in each factor. A few of them were ranked differently. 'Participation in economic trade groups' ranked as LESS IMPORTANT for high profit/low risk companies. The reason might be the low risk in suppliers. Since companies do not experience any risks in finding the suppliers, 'participation in economic trade groups' may not be so important for them. On the contrary, two of the low risk companies in the case study sample underlined the importance of the trade agreements. Thus, this factor also incorporates the effect of the other variables.

QUALITY OF LIFE

There are differences among the groups. However, they cannot be explained with the product strategy choice of the companies.

Summary of the Results for Variable IV: Product Strategy

Table 26 is the summary table for product strategy. Four variables (high profit/high risk, high profit/low risk, low profit/low risk, low profit/high risk) are put in each column in the table and factor groups are placed in the rows. Three sections (must, highly recommended and optional) are divided by dotted lines.

Table 25 Summary table for product strategy

		High profit / High risk	High profit / Low risk	Low profit / Low risk
Cost	*Must*	Total Cost of Product Participation in economic trade groups Tax	Total Cost of Product Participation in economic trade groups Quota Cost Government Incentives Tax	Total Cost of Product Quota Cost Government Incentives Land Cost Transaction Cost Tax
	Highly recommended	Quota Cost Land Cost Transaction Cost Government Incentives	Land Cost	
	Optional			Participation in economic trade groups
Availability	*Must*	Availability of transportation Availability of infrastructure Availability of suppliers Availability of middle management Availability of skilled labor Availability of new markets Availability of raw materials Availability of technology Availability of capital	Availability of transportation Availability of infrastructure Availability of suppliers Availability of middle management Availability of raw materials Bargaining power of suppliers Availability of technology Availability of capital Availability of incentives	Availability of transportation Availability of infrastructure Availability of suppliers Availability of middle management Availability of capital Availability of skilled labor Availability of incentives
	Highly recommended	Bargaining power of suppliers	Availability of lending institutions Availability of new markets Availability of skilled labor	Availability of raw materials Availability of new markets
	Optional	Availability of incentives Availability of lending institutions		Availability of technology Availability of lending institutions
Accessibility	*Must*	Lead Time Proximity to markets Proximity to suppliers Demographics of industry	Lead Time Proximity to markets Proximity to suppliers Flexibility of production Demographics of industry	Lead Time Proximity to markets Proximity to suppliers
	Highly recommended	Flexibility of production		Demographics of industry
	Optional			Flexibility of production
Quality	*Must*	Quality of Product Environmental standards Ethical standards	Quality of Product Environmental standards Ethical standards	Quality of Product Environmental standards Ethical standards

Table 26 (con't)

		High profit / High risk	High profit / Low risk	Low profit / Low risk
Risk/Uncertainty	Must	Delivery Reliability Political Stability Currency Stability Inflation Rate Income Trends Population trends Interest Rate National content laws of the country Location of the competitors	Delivery Reliability Political Stability Currency Stability Inflation Rate Banking system stability Labor Unions Income Trends Population trends Interest Rate National content laws of the country	Delivery Reliability Political Stability Currency Stability Inflation Rate Labor Unions Income Trends Population trends Interest Rate
	Highly recommended	Labor Unions Banking system stability	Location of the competitors	
	Optional			Location of the competitors Banking system stability National content laws of the country
Ease of operations	Must	Participation in economic trade groups Corporate investment rules Taxation of foreign owned companies Legal systems Export/Import Regulations Regulations MJV Ownership rights	Regulations MJV Taxation of foreign owned companies Ownership rights Legal systems Export/Import Regulations	Corporate investment rules Regulations MJV Taxation of foreign owned companies Legal systems Participation in economic trade groups Export/Import Regulations
	Highly recommended		Participation in economic trade groups Corporate investment rules	
	Optional			Ownership rights
Quality of Life	Must	Cost of living Per capita income	Cost of living Per capita income	Cost of living
	Highly recommended	Availability of universities, colleges Temperature	Temperature Availability of universities, colleges	Temperature
	Optional			Per capita income Availability of universities, colleges

Research Objective 2: To determine the effect of organizational culture on location factors

Organizational culture was defined in the literature as the following three variables:

- Risk taking behavior of companies
- Autonomy in terms of information sharing practice in the company
- Involvement level in the final decision for international investments

However, only the 'risk taking behavior' of the companies is examined in this section. The initial development of the conceptual model included the remaining two variables, which have direct effects on the investment decisions, however, a systemic approach to collect data for these variables were found to be too complex and beyond the scope of this study.

Variable I: Risk Taking Behavior

More than one-third of the respondents (35%, n=17) indicated that their companies would be considered take low-risks takers. This percentage increases to 59% when the risk level is measured as medium risk takers. Only one company (6%, n=17) mentioned that it would take high risks. Since only one respondent considered their companies to be high-risk takers, the remaining discussion consists of the responses by the medium and low risk companies.

Table 26 The distribution of the survey and case study results for risk taking behavior of companies

	High Risks	Medium Risks	Low Risks	TOTAL
Survey Results	1	10	6	17
Case Study Results	-	4	2	6

In reviewing the responses from the case study interviews, only one company mentioned that they made a conscious effort to lower or reduce their risk-taking behavior. "We used to take high risks in the past," said one of the executives, "now we are calculating every scenario and make decisions based on these calculated risks."

Location factors

COST

Although there are no statistically proven differences between the two risk types and the variables used to measure cost, the medium-risk companies generally ranked cost factors of 'Total Cost Of Product', 'Participation In Trade Groups', and 'Land Cost' as MORE IMPORTANT than did the low-risk group. Surprisingly, the low-risk companies ranked 'Participation in Trade Groups' as LESS IMPORTANT, and but 'Quota Costs' and 'Government Incentives' as MORE IMPORTANT." This ranking for the low-risk respondent companies appears contradictory, in that most, trade groups are usually proponents of fair trade and support incentive packages that facilitate trade. It would be assumed that those seeking to take the lowest risk would use these organizations as clearinghouses of the latest trade information or to assist their company in finding "best practice' paradigms for business.

AVAILABILITY

As expected, every factor in this category was rated as MORE IMPORTANT by medium risk companies than by the low risk ones (Figure 31). The reason might be

149

medium-risk companies' paying more attention to the availability of factors than the low- risk companies.

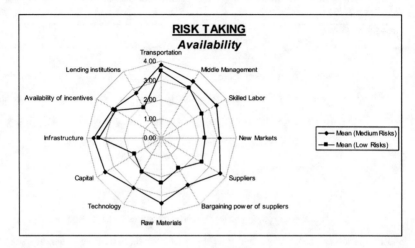

Figure 28 Mean comparisons of the location factors under availability category according to the risk taking behaviors of companies

ACCESSIBILITY

As expected, nearly every factor in this category was rated as MORE IMPORTANT by medium risk companies than by the low risk ones. 'Lead time' and 'proximity to markets' and 'proximity to suppliers' factors were equally IMPORTANT for each group.

QUALITY

Factors in the 'quality' group were ranked as VERY IMPORTANT for every group for product strategy.

RISK/UNCERTAINTY

Interestingly, there did not appear a difference in the ranking of the factors. Low risk groups still rated them lower, but there is not a big difference between ratings. Only 'income trends', banking system stability' and 'location of the competitors' factors were ranked low in the low risk group rankings. Companies may consider every factor at the beginning of their decision making process, however, their moves may differ at the end.

EASE OF OPERATIONS

'Export/import regulations', 'legal systems', and 'taxation of foreign owned companies' are the important factors for both groups in this category. For other factors, the expected difference mentioned above is still valid.

QUALITY OF LIFE

There is the above-mentioned difference between the groups. 'Cost of living' is the most important factor.

Summary of the Results for Variable I: Risk Taking Behavior

Table 27 is the summary table for risk taking behaviors of companies. Two variables (medium risks and low risks) are put in each column in the table and factor groups are placed in the rows. Three sections (must, highly recommended and optional) are divided by dotted lines.

Table 27 Summary table for risk taking behavior of companies

		Medium Risks	Low Risks
Cost	*Must*	Total Cost of Product Participation in economic trade groups Transaction Cost Tax Government Incentives Land Cost	Total Cost of Product Quota Cost Government Incentives Transaction Cost Tax Land Cost
	Highly recommended	Quota Cost	Participation in economic trade groups
	Optional		
Availability	*Must*	Availability of transportation Availability of infrastructure Availability of suppliers Availability of middle management Availability of skilled labor Availability of new markets Availability of raw materials Availability of technology Bargaining power of suppliers Availability of incentives Availbility of lending institutions Availability of capital	Availability of transportation Availability of infrastructure Availability of middle management Availability of incentives
	Highly recommended		Availability of skilled labor Availability of new markets Availability of suppliers Availability of raw materials
	Optional		Bargaining power of suppliers Availability of technology Availability of capital Availability of lending institutions
Accessibility	*Must*	Lead Time Proximity to markets Proximity to suppliers Demographics of industry	Lead Time Proximity to markets Proximity to suppliers Flexibility of production
	Highly recommended	Flexibility of production	Demographics of industry
	Optional		
Quality	*Must*	Quality of Product Environmental standards Ethical standards	Quality of Product Environmental standards Ethical standards

Table 27 (con't)

		Medium Risks	Low Risks
Risk/Uncertainty	*Must*	Labor Unions Income Trends Population trends Location of the competitors Delivery Reliability Political Stability Currency Stability Inflation Rate Banking system stability Interest Rate National content laws of the country	Labor Unions Population trends Delivery Reliability Political Stability Currency Stability Inflation Rate Interest Rate National content laws of the country
	Highly recommended		Income Trends Banking system stability
	Optional		Location of the competitors
Ease of operations	*Must*	Participation in economic trade groups Corporate investment rules Taxation of foreign owned companies Legal systems Export/Import Regulations Regulations MJV Ownership rights	Regulations MJV Taxation of foreign owned companies Legal systems Export/Import Regulations
	Highly recommended		Corporate Investment Rules Participation in economic trade groups Ownership rights
	Optional		
Quality of Life	*Must*	Cost of living Per capita income Availability of universities, colleges	Cost of living
	Highly recommended		
	Optional	Temperature	Per capita income Temperature Availability of universities, colleges

153

Research Objective 3: To determine the effect of the sector type on location factors

Variable I: Sector Type

Four types of sectors are considered in this research:

- Fiber (n=2)
- Textiles (n=10)
- Apparel (n=7)
- Nonwovens (n=2)

Although there are 17 responses, some companies categorized themselves under two categories. The responses of these companies are duplicated to the second sector that they put themselves in. Because of this reason, the total increased to 21.

Location factors

COST

One explainable difference is in the 'land cost' factor (Figure 29). Since the likelihood of greenfield operations in apparel group is very low, land cost is less important for that group. Again, since they consider sourcing in most of the times, quota cost is relatively MORE IMPORTANT for them than for the other groups. An additional factor was mentioned during a case study interview. One of the executives of an apparel company mentioned the 'training rebates' for labor as an IMPORTANT factor. Since apparel sector is a labor-intensive sector, this factor makes sense for apparel companies.

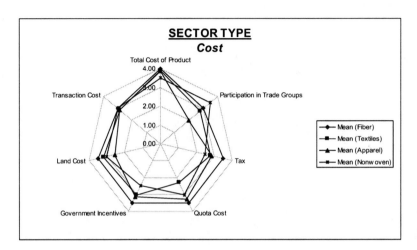

Figure 29 Mean comparisons of the location factors under cost category according to the sector type

AVAILABILITY

'Availability of new markets' appeared to be IMPORTANT for fibers and textiles companies whereas others ranked this factor as less important (Figure 30). The reason may depend on the eagerness of the fiber and textile companies to enter new markets. For example, Asia is a big market for fiber companies nowadays. One of the executives mentioned that most of the production in fiber sector has shifted to Asia to supply the textile companies (their customers) who have already been there for years. Apparel companies, on the other hand, still consider the US market as their primary target market. That's why they do not consider new markets as a very IMPORTANT factor. This result is also supported by the case study results. Four out of six companies mentioned the importance of this factor.

155

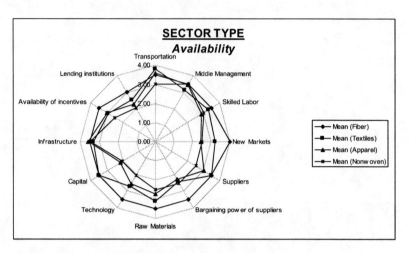

Figure 30 Mean comparisons of the location factors under availability category according to the sector type

Most of the companies ranked 'availability of technology' as LESS IMPORTANT. They, most of the time, own the technology or can provide the technology easily to the foreign operations due to their strong capital reserves.

ACCESIBILITY

Most important factors are 'lead time', flexibility of production' and 'proximity to suppliers' for nearly all of the sectors (Figure 31).

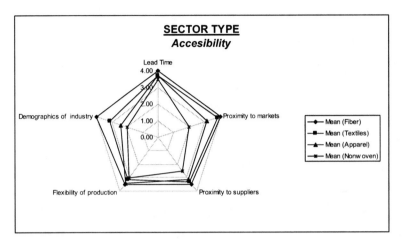

Figure 31 Mean comparisons of the location factors under accessibility category according to the sector type

QUALITY

All of the companies ranked these factors as VERY IMPORTANT both in the survey and in the case study results.

RISK/UNCERTAINTY

'Political stability' and 'delivery reliability' factors were the MOST IMPORTANT factors for every sector. Apparel companies did not consider their competitors' behavior as an important factor. Nonwoven companies took fewer factors into consideration than the other sectors.

EASE OF OPERATIONS

'Taxation of foreign owned companies', export/import regulations' and 'legal systems' were the IMPORTANT factors in this category. It was interesting to see that apparel companies ranked 'participation in economic trade groups' as less important.

This result does not reflect the usual behavior of the apparel companies. They did not consider the corporate investment rules as an important factor. This may be because of the growth strategy that they follow. Most of the time, they prefer either the strategic partnership or sourcing as a growth strategy. However, this factor is more important for greenfield operation strategists than the rest.

QUALITY OF LIFE

There were differences among the groups. However, they cannot be explained with the sector type of the companies.

Summary of the Results for Variable I: Sector Type

Table 28 is the summary table for sector type. Four variables (fiber, textile, apparel, nonwoven) are put in each column in the table and factor groups are placed in the rows. Three sections (must, highly recommended and optional) are divided by dotted lines.

Table 28 Summary table of sector type

		Fiber	Textile	Apparel
Cost	*Must*	Total Cost of Product	Total Cost of Product	Total Cost of Product
		Participation in economic trade groups	Participation in economic trade groups	Quota Cost
		Transaction Cost	Land Cost	Government Incentives
		Tax	Government Incentives	Transaction Cost
		Land Cost	Transaction Cost	Tax
		Goverment Incentives	Tax	
		Quota Cost		
	Highly recommended	Quota Cost		Land Cost
	Optional		Quota Cost	Participation in economic trade groups
Availability	*Must*	Availability of transportation	Availability of transportation	Availability of transportation
		Availability of infrastructure	Availability of infrastructure	Availability of infrastructure
		Availability of suppliers	Availability of suppliers	Availability of suppliers
		Availability of middle management	Availability of middle management	Availability of middle management
		Availability of skilled labor	Availability of raw materials	Availability of skilled labor
		Bargaining power of suppliers	Availability of capital	Availability of incentives
		Availability of raw materials	Availability of incentives	Availability of new markets
		Availability of technology	Availability of new markets	Availability of raw materials
		Availability of capital		
		Availability of incentives		
		Availability of lending institutions		
	Highly recommended	Availability of new markets	Availability of lending institutions	Availability of technology
			Availability of technology	
			Availability of skilled labor	
	Optional		Bargaining power of suppliers	Bargaining power of suppliers
				Availability of lending institutions
				Availability of capital
Accessibility	*Must*	Lead Time	Lead Time	Lead Time
		Proximity to markets	Proximity to markets	Proximity to markets
		Proximity to suppliers	Proximity to suppliers	Proximity to suppliers
		Demographics of industry	Flexibility of production	Flexibility of production
		Flexibility of production	Demographics of industry	
	Highly recommended			
	Optional			Demographics of industry

Table 28 (con't)

		Fiber	Textile	Apparel
Quality	*Must*	Quality of Product Environmental standards Ethical standards	Quality of Product Environmental standards Ethical standards	Quality of Product Environmental standards Ethical standards
Risk/Uncertainty	*Must*	Delivery Reliability Political Stability Currency Stability Inflation Rate Labor Unions Income Trends Population trends Interest Rate National content laws of the country Location of the competitors Banking system stability	Delivery Reliability Political Stability Currency Stability Inflation Rate Banking system stability Labor Unions Income Trends Population trends Interest Rate National content laws of the country Location of competitors	Delivery Reliability Political Stability Currency Stability Inflation Rate Labor Unions Population trends Interest Rate National content laws of the country Banking system stability
	Highly recommended			Income trends
	Optional			Location of the competitors
Ease of operations	*Must*	Participation in economic trade groups Corporate investment rules Taxation of foreign owned companies Legal systems Export/Import Regulations Regulations MJV Ownership rights	Regulations MJV Taxation of foreign owned companies Ownership rights Legal systems Export/Import Regulations Participation in economic trade groups Corporate investment rules	Regulations MJV Taxation of foreign owned companies Legal systems Export/Import Regulations
	Highly recommended			Corporate investment rules
	Optional			Participation in economic trade groups Ownership rights
Quality of Life	*Must*	Cost of living Per capita income Temperature Availability of universities, colleges	Cost of living Availability of universities, colleges	Cost of living
	Highly recommended		Per capita income	Per capita income Availability of universities, colleges
	Optional	Temperature	Temperature	Temperature

DISCUSSION

This section discusses the importance of location factors according to the research objectives. For each objective, only the major differences and group responses are provided.

Research Objective 1: To determine the effect of strategy on location factors

Variable I: Corporate Strategy

When the responses of the survey were grouped according the respondents' self-identification of their corporate strategy, the major differences among the three strategist groups were for 6 of the 7 sub-variables (cost, availability, accessibility, risk/uncertainty, ease of operation, quality of life).

Cost

Although every group selected the factor 'total cost of product' as VERY IMPORTANT, there are differences in their rankings of other the cost factors (e.g., quota cost, government incentives. Based on the results, all companies appear to be more aware of the importance of the 'total cost of product' overall, not just these individual parts of cost as in the past. Although they are aware of these contributory direct cost factors, results showed that according to their corporate strategy, companies may not be realizing the importance of the cost drivers like 'quota cost' and 'participation in economic trade group' as individual contributors of cost. This is notable because although these types of factors do not seem to affect the cost of the product directly, eventually they increase or decrease the total cost value for a product. Therefore, companies should intensely consider all of the factors under this category and the ideal ranking for all of the cost factors would be VERY IMPORANT.

Availability

In this group, the major differences were in the 'availability of new markets', 'availability of raw materials', and 'availability of skilled labor' factors. 'Availability of new markets' is discussed under the assumption that focus and differentiation strategists are mostly making international investments based on the marketing strategies, and cost leaders are making the investments mainly concerning the cost strategies. Based on the limited responses, this assumption may not be true, in general. A cost leader also can have a concern of locating and entering new markets and can decide to make international investments to accomplish their cost leadership objective.

In terms of recommendations based on the results, 'availability of raw materials' should be considered as VERY IMPORTANT. In addition, 'bargaining power of supplier' should at least be considered as IMPORTANT for cost leaders. The rankings of the differentiators and focus strategists appear to be consistent with their objective and the findings in the literature.

Accessibility

For this factor, there were differences among the strategists in the weighting of two factors: 'flexibility of the product' and 'demographics of the industry'. Ideally, differentiators should be more concerned about the 'flexibility of the product' factor and this was the result of the survey. Regarding the 'demographics of the industry', this factor should be ranked higher in importance, for cost leaders, because it can affect the total cost of the product. For instance, if the location that company has selected to invest in is not located inside their existing network of suppliers, the company may incur additional expenses to transport the raw material to the primary location, or in the most extreme situation, the company would locate a new facility to capture the advantages of

162

using the non-network supplier. This extra effort would ultimately increase the "total cost of the product". Plus, being part of the network for an industry in a country can provide special incentives like access to regional capital sources and economic incentive zones to the company.

Risk/Uncertainty

Of the 11 factors for this group, 'Location of competitors' was the only one ranked differently among the strategists. However, regardless of the strategy, companies should pay attention to what their competitors are doing. Thus, ideally, this factor should be rated as VERY IMPORTANT.

When this factor was discussed with interviewees for the case studies, an additional factor, 'country culture', appeared to be important. This factor includes the local people's working principles, government's way of doing business and moral in the processes. If companies find difficulties to deal with the differences in the country culture, they may experience hard times in the manufacturing process due to the labor inclusion to these processes. Therefore, 'country culture' should be included under risk/uncertainty category in the list in future studies of international investment decisions.

Although companies mentioned that they pay attention to the factors like income trends, population trends, and economic stability. The legitimacy of this argument is questionable after the case studies. Most of the companies do not have a database or a space to store data about countries. Therefore, it is questionable how strongly they are concerned about these data.

Ease of Operations

'Participation in economic trade groups' appeared as a less important factor for focus and differentiator strategists. It is discussed in the results section that it may be due to the motivation of the companies. They are motivated towards marketing side than the cost side. However, 'participation in an economic trade group' brings advantages in both ways, companies may gain access to other countries more easily due to this factor. Therefore, it should be, ideally, considered as very important.

Quality of Life

'Per capita income' appeared as an UNIMPORTANT factor for cost leaders; however, it indirectly reflects the cost figures of the country. Therefore, in the ideal table, this factor is put into the 'highly recommended' section for cost leaders.

Variable II: Growth Strategy

In this variable, there was no distinct prioritization of the location factors among the sub-variables for the three types of growth strategies (greenfield, strategic partnerships, and sourcing). However, it was expected to see some differences in the rankings of the factors since some factors mostly serve to the needs of greenfield operations, like land cost, government incentives, taxation of the foreign-owned companies, and ownership rights. Although these factors are not totally unique to greenfield operations, it was expected that greenfield operation strategists would rank these the factors as more important than other two strategist types.

Variable III: Operational Strategy

No major difference for rankings occurred based on grouping the location factors for international investment decisions according to the operational strategies.

Variable IV: Product Strategy

Only two location factors (cost and availability) appeared to have notable differences in the ranking of their sub-variables were grouped according the respondents self-identification of the product strategy for their company.

Cost

"High profit" group does not aggressively take into account the cost factors. Their prioritization is mostly on market related factors. For this reason, in the ideal table, most of the cost factors are put under 'highly recommended' list. The "Low profit" group has already ranked all of the cost factors in the 'must' list.

Availability

For the high supplier risk group, 'bargaining power of suppliers' should be as important as 'proximity to suppliers'. It should be even more important than that factor since it would be very critical for company to look for other suppliers or to bargain with them if the bargaining power of suppliers is high. Thus, in the ideal table, this factor is put to the 'must' category for high profit/high risk group.

It may be effective for low profit group to consider the 'availability of raw materials' factor more seriously. This factor may provide them an advantage in terms of profit generation. Thus, in the ideal table, this factor is put to the 'must' section.

Research Objective 2: To determine the effect of organizational culture on location factors

Variable I: Risk Taking Behavior

Grouping seven factors according to the respondents' self-identification of organization culture yielded no major differences among the 4 types of cultures. One notable recommended change would be to reclassify the 'quota cost' factor to the 'must' section for medium risks since they should concern this cost factor due to their medium risk taking practice.

Research Objective 3: To determine the effect of the sector type on location factors

Variable I: Sector Type

When the responses of the survey were grouped according the respondents' self-identification of their sector, the major differences among the four sectors were for 2 of the 7 sub-variables (cost, availability, accessibility, risk/uncertainty, ease of operation, quality of life).

Cost

The discussion in the cost section of the corporate strategy variable is also valid for this section. Every cost factor should be important for every sector. For this reason, in the ideal table, all of them are put in the 'must' section.

Availability

For fiber sector, availability of new markets factor is important. In the case study discussions, executives mentioned that market dynamics are changing and mostly shifting towards Asia. Given this fact, companies should consider this factor more seriously. Therefore, in the ideal table, this factor is put in the must section.

166

For nonwoven sector, 'availability of technology' factor might be important since it is a technology intensive sector. It is a fact that most of the companies consider moving the current technology that they already have to a new location. Still, availability of technology incorporates also the technical support. Therefore, this factor should be put at least in the highly recommended section. 'Proximity to markets' factor is also put into the highly recommended section based on the case study results. One of the executives mentioned that the only reason to invest for them was to be close to their markets. Therefore, it is clear that at least some attention should be given to this factor.

Ease of operations

For apparel companies, 'participation in economic trade groups' factor is in the 'optional' section based on the quantitative results. However, it is a very important factor especially for apparel companies according to the interviews that have been performed. Most of the companies are conducting sourcing operations as international investments and special regulations create an advantage for this type of investment.

CONCLUSIONS

Globalization influenced international production and trade in a great extent. This influence originated with the trade agreements among different countries or different parts of the world. Companies started to think globally. This mindset requires seeing the world as the operation field and investing in any part of it if it creates a competitive advantage for the company. In this respect, this paper aimed to understand the decision-making process of the textile and apparel companies for international investment decisions. The effect of internal environment of a company was analyzed on the international investment decisions using a survey and a case study research methodology. The research sample for survey implementation comprised 17 companies from fiber, textile, apparel and nonwovens sectors. To support the limited survey

167

results, case studies were conducted with 6 companies. Following research objectives were investigated for textile and apparel companies:

RO1: To determine the effect of strategy on location factors

- Corporate strategy

- Specific operational strategy

- Product strategy

- Growth strategy

RO2: To determine the effect of organizational culture on location factors

RO3: To determine the effect of the sector type on location factors

Each variable used under these categories were assumed to be independent. For example, when considering a cost leader company, the effect of its being a fiber company was not taken into account.

The 'Customized Investment Decisions Tool', which was discussed in Part IV, was used as the instrument of the survey and case studies. The tool consists of 49 location factors divided into seven categories. The categories are: cost, availability, accessibility, quality, risk/uncertainty, ease of operations and quality of life.

Research Objective 1:

In overall, the effect of corporate strategy and product strategy were identified through survey results. Growth strategy and specific operational strategy did not appear as very important in determining the importance levels of the location factors.

Corporate Strategy

For corporate strategy category, there appeared differences considering the special center of attentions of the strategists. In general, there was an apparent difference between the choices of cost leadership strategists and the rest of the strategists (differentiators and focus strategists). Both direct and indirect cost were the focal point of the cost leaders for international investments; whereas, it changes to new markets and products when differentiators and focus (niche) strategists concerned. The difference between the differentiators and the focus group was the degree of importance most of the time. This understandable since the main difference between a focus strategist and a differentiator is the size of the market most of the time (Porter, 1980).

Cost leaders, as expected, were very much concerned about the cost factors, and availability and accessibility factors that would indirectly affect cost as a result like availability of transportation and proximity to suppliers. The quota cost factor was an exception in this case. Cost leaders did not consider this factor as important. However, for a larger sample, the expectation is it will be considered as very important for cost leaders.

Differentiation strategists either try to differentiate their product line or the services that they offer. This fact leads them to have concerns about the flexibility of production factor, which supports the aim of differentiating their products. Most of the risk/uncertainty factors were more important for them than the cost factors. This finding is again because of their marketing focus for international investments than a cost focus.

Focus (niche) strategists either concentrate in the market or the product. Therefore, 'availability of markets' and 'proximity to customers/markets' factors were important for them. Since the market that they serve, most of the time, is relatively dense and small, 'location of the competitors' factor was also important in addition to the above factors.

Specifically, the 'participation in economic trade groups' was more important to cost leaders than the other strategists due to the nature of the strategy. Again differentiation and focus group do not concentrate that much on the cost factors for international investment decisions. And 'per capita income' was more important for the differentiators and focus strategists for the quality of life category since a new location might mean a new opportunity for them to market their products, so the buying power in the country appeared to be important.

Product Strategy

Products were mainly classified according to the supplier risk that they encompass and the profit margin that they offer. In general, companies with products that can only generate **low profit** were more concern about the cost factors. **High profit** products are usually the specialty and niche products. Companies with these types of products were not particularly very much concerned about the cost factors. Their attention was more on the new markets. This consequence is explicable since the potential size of the market of these types of products is limited.

High supplier risk in products channeled the companies to consider the factors like 'availability of suppliers' and 'proximity to suppliers'. Specifically for low profit/ low risk products, companies did not consider the 'participation in economic trade groups' factor. This may be due to the **low risk** in suppliers. If there is plethora of suppliers available, they may not, specifically, chase the countries with special trade agreements.

Research Objective 2:

The effect of organizational culture is determined by analyzing the risk taking behavior of companies. In overall, **low risk takers** ranked most of the factors as more important than the medium to **high risk takers**.

Research Objective 3:

Companies in four sectors are surveyed: **fiber, textile, apparel** and **nonwoven**. When the characteristics of the sectors are recalled, fiber, textile and nonwoven sector is a capital intensive sector, whereas the apparel sector is labor intensive. Besides, nonwoven sector specifically requires more attention in high

170

technology than others. Another difference appears when their sequence in the supply chain is concerned. Fiber, textile and apparel is the regular sequence of the supply chain. Nonwoven sector is also a supplier at the same level as textiles since their products are also used as a part of end product most of the time.

Based on the survey and case study results, fiber and textile companies mostly consider the greenfield operations and strategic partnerships, whereas, apparel companies consider strategic partnerships and sourcing as their growth strategy. Although a difference did not appear in the growth strategy discussion part of this study, the effect revealed itself in this part. In terms of cost factors, 'land cost' is ranked as less important for apparel companies than the rest.

The main finding in this section is the importance of the new markets for fiber, textile and nonwoven companies than the apparel companies. The reason of this importance is due to the position of these sectors in the supply chain. Most of the apparel companies already moved to overseas and started doing partnerships with foreign companies. This move has affected the market share of the fiber and textile companies in the US. The US fiber and textile companies started to conduct international investments in the same countries where their customers (apparel producers) have moved. In this way, they found a chance to compete with their foreign competitors and they were able to sustain their market share. Therefore, 'availability of new markets' and 'proximity to markets/customers' factors were very important for fiber and textile companies.

In conclusion, based on the survey and case study results, it is proved that the strategy, organization culture and sector type of a company have effects on the international investment decisions. However, due to the limited number of responses, these results may not be representative for the whole population.

REFERENCES

Dillman, D. A. (2000). <u>Mail and Internet Surveys: The Tailored Design Method</u> (second ed.). Canada: John Wiley & Sons Inc.

Heisler, E. (2003, March 16, 2003). Struggle: South of the border; the textile experiment in Mexico showed promise, but problems piled up quickly. Ultimately, corporate mistakes and economic misfortunes led to failures. <u>The News & Record</u>.

Porter, M. (1980). <u>Competitive Strategy Techniques for analyzing industries and competitors</u>. New York: The Free Press.

172

Part VI: A Strategic Model For International Investment Decisions

INTRODUCTION

Internationalization efforts of textile and apparel companies across the world have generated riskier business/market environments, since the market that they operate in under constant change. These companies now have to control for more complex operations and complicated relationships among operations than in the past. This control is hard since not only the internal capabilities of the organization have to be considered, but the external factors have effects on the success of the control.

Investment decisions form the backbone of the internationalization process. Companies invest in international locations to gain either a manufacturing advantage or a marketing advantage. However, there always exists the possibility of failure due to long term and short term uncertainty in the environment. Companies made international investment decisions according to several different ways. Some companies only focused on the generic objective of lowering costs without even considering if this objective supported their overall objectives. Others considered some countries without examining the macro-level performance of the countries (Heisler, 2003). The country may offer significant advantages to a company; however, it is always critical to analyze both the advantages and the disadvantages. If the culture of a country, for example, is an obstacle for a company to operate with its organizational values and its own way of doing business, the advantages may be hindered in the long term. Therefore, companies have to be aware of the multi-criteria nature of the investment decisions including both the internal environment criteria and the external environment criteria.

In considering, external and internal environments, external environment defined as the business environment where company operates. The macro level factors including economic, social, political, legal, technological factors, and micro level factors including customers, competitors, and suppliers in countries are the main consideration of companies (Kotler, 2003). In international investment decisions, focus on external environment represents considering the location factors of the countries. Focus on

174

internal environment, on the other hand, represents the concentration on the objectives, organizational values, beliefs, short and long term strategies of the company.

There are different practices in the real world. Some companies only consider the external environment whereas others concentrate on the internal environment. The literature about these different practices is examined in this paper. The real world experience is collected through an empirical study with the textile and apparel industry (Part V). Based on the findings, a strategic model, which considers both the internal environment and the external environment of the company, is then developed for international investments. This approach provides a full guide to healthy investment decisions.

LITERATURE REVIEW

Literature was reviewed based on the following categorization:

- Focus on internal environment
- Focus on external environment
- Focus on both internal and external environment

Focus on Internal Environment

Schemenner (1979) is a well-known researcher in plant location area. He mainly focused on the internal environment and suggested that companies must identify their needs thoroughly before analyzing different countries. He mentioned that the actual selection of a new plant site should be conducted concerning (Schmenner, 1979):

- A company's capacity needs
- The extent and quality of its present capacity
- The way in which its existing plants fit together in a multi-plant manufacturing strategy
- Expected future demands on manufacturing, apart from mere space requirements

Schmenner (1979) also emphasized the importance of assigning a strategic role to the plant and stated that many companies found themselves owning vacant tracts of land and were often seeking ways to fill them up. "Too often the idea is 'What can we put at that site?' rather than 'What site makes sense for this product, market or technology?'"(Schmenner, 1979). The plant strategies are based on the purpose of the plants:

- Product Plant Strategy: the main objective is to manufacture a specific product
- Market Area plant strategy: the main objective is to be able to enter a new market
- Product-Market Plant strategy: this strategy includes both manufacturing a specific product and entering a new market as objectives
- Process Plant strategy: the main objectives is to conduct a specific process
- General Purpose plant strategy: the main objective might be to expand the capacity

Another example for internal focus is the study of Govindarajan and Gupta (2001). They suggested companies develop a global mindset before starting an operation internationally. They emphasized that companies should transform themselves into a global knowledge machine. Companies have to develop an effective knowledge management to be successful globally (Govindarajan & Gupta, 2001).

Brush, Maritan and Karnani (1999) conducted a study that focused on mostly the internal environment. They developed a framework and empirically investigated the combined importance of international business and manufacturing strategy literature for the plant location choice of the firm. International business represented with one dimension of being a foreign or a domestic company (US). Manufacturing strategy was defined as the choice between locating an independent versus an integrated plant (Brush et al., 1999). Although, they analyzed the location factors based on the manufacturing strategy of the companies, their 'strategy' definition is not that broad.

176

Besides, other than the categorization of the factors for foreign and domestic firms, there was not a real focus on the external environment. Still, the idea of trying to interpret and categorize the location factors according to the manufacturing strategy of the company was a valuable contribution to the literature. Considering the external environment was also valuable.

Focus on External Environment

Focus on external environment simply represents considering only the location factors without considering company's own needs and interests, and its organizational culture. Most of the researchers concentrated on the categorization of the location factors according to the type of the industry disregarding company level intensity. A more detailed analysis for external environment was suggested by the president and fellows of Harvard College in 1989. They considered the list of factors affecting facility location decisions as relatively constant, however they argued the importance or weighting of the factors could vary greatly by industry, product life cycle and facility type (Notes on Facility, 1989) Emphasizing the significance of the three dimensions; industry type, product life cycle stage and facility type while determining the importance of each factor is a valuable contribution to the literature.

Focus on both Internal and External Environment

MacCormack, Newmand and Rosenfield (1994) focused both on the external environment and the internal environment. They argued that traditional approaches of focusing strictly on cost factors no longer applied and large, centralized manufacturing facilities in low cost countries with poorly skilled workers were not sustainable. They claimed that the trend was to a more decentralized manufacturing structure with smaller, lower-scale plants serving demand in regional markets. This argument, which was claimed in 1994, is still not valid for every type of decision today. Locating

177

manufacturing facilities overseas is still an effective practice if conducted properly. However, the framework that they suggested is worth analyzing (MacCormack, Newman, & Rosenfield, 1994):

Phase 1: Establish the critical success factors of the business, the degree of global orientation necessary, and the required manufacturing support role.

Phase 2: Assess options for regional manufacturing configuration, considering market access, risk management, customer demand characteristics, and the impact of production technologies on plant scale.

Phase 3:Define a set of potential sites, primarily based on infrastructure, that adequately supports the business and manufacturing strategies.

Phase 4: Rank the most cost effective solutions, using a quantitative analysis of remaining location options, and define the manner of operation.

In this framework, the first two phases concentrate on the internal environment and the last two concentrates on the analysis of the external environment.

Bartmess and Cerny (1993) criticized the traditional location analyses with complex mathematical models that determine the location, which minimizes a firm's total cost by balancing such elements as factor costs, transportation costs, and taxes. They proposed a conceptual model for plant location decisions, which considers the critical capabilities of companies rather than cost factors. They stated that companies should identify their critical capabilities and make the plant location analysis to get the most benefit from the proposed countries based on their critical capabilities. In other words, the objective of the plant location analysis should be to identify the network that combines these benefits in such a way that the net present value of future cash flows to the company is maximized. (Bartmess & Cerny, 1993)

Vos (1997) concentrated on this type of companies and proposed a design method to structure and support their international manufacturing and logistics structure. Proposed method included the identification of the problem as a first stage. Then plant location analysis and alternative location generation form the design stage,

178

and in the selection stage an evaluation of the locations is performed. This strategic approach interrogates the decision of locating an additional capacity, if plant location will be a solution to the problem in the identification stage or not. After this decision, system evaluates countries according to different factors stated (Vos, 1997).

Solely an external focus is insufficient to make the right decision. Both Bartmess and Cerny (1993) and MacCormack, Newman and Rosenfield (1994) stated that the financial benefits from relocating to a low cost country were nearly immediate, but they were all too often transitory. Therefore, companies should focus on both the internal and the external environment to be able to make effective international investments.

A STRATEGIC MODEL

A strategic model was developed based on the literature review and the findings from survey and case study results of Part V. The variables that have proven effects on the international investment decisions were taken into consideration in the model. This strategic model, which considers both:

- o the internal environment of the company by questioning the strategy, the organizational culture, and sector type of the company, and
- o the external environment of the company by considering the important location factors

is presented in Figure 32.

First, the sections of the model are explained. Then, the logic of the model is explained in the second part of the discussion.

Sections of the Model

The model has five sections:

1. Internal Environment Analysis

2. International Investment Plan

3. Location Factors Selection

4. External Environment Analysis

5. Solution Generator

Internal Environment Analysis

Companies have to analyze themselves before starting the actual investment investigation. First, they have to determine or recall their critical success factors or core capabilities. This determination enables their understanding of the whole picture.

Companies should act to enhance their core capabilities or to gain supporting capabilities with the aid of different locations. For example, if manufacturing is the core capability of a company, locating manufacturing away from the headquarters where coordination might not be good enough can diminish or even destroy the core capability.

On the contrary, if one locates its manufacturing core capability to a place where the competitive advantage of the company strengthens, it might be a good move for the company. Thus, companies have to know their core capabilities.

Second, companies have to determine/recall their strategic objectives. Strategic objectives give the direction of which way the company will move to stay competitive in the environment. International investment decisions have to support the company's long-term direction. If the investment decision does not support the overall objectives of the company, the investment will generate no use for the company. In addition, since international investment requires tremendous amount of time and money, company will lose a lot from that investment. Therefore, determining the strategic objectives of the company is critical.

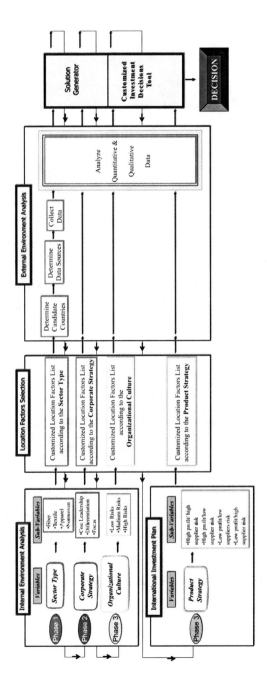

Figure 32 A strategic model for international investments

175

The preferences of companies for their internal environment influence the whole process of decision-making. Internal environment is defined by three variables based on the literature review and survey and case study research:

- Sector Type
- Corporate Strategy
- Organizational Culture

The fact of being a fiber company, choosing a differentiation strategy and having a low risk taking behavior can lead the company toward a different path from being an apparel company, choosing a focus strategy and having a high risk taking behavior in international investment decisions. Therefore, companies have to be aware of their internal environments' needs to be able to have a customized decision making process according to these needs. As a result, this self-assessment step is very important for companies to construct the right basis and understanding among the decision makers. Companies will be aware of their self-interests at the end of this step.

International Investment Plan

This section could still be considered under the internal environment analysis since it is still a part of the internal environment of the company. However, the investment plan changes from decision to decision. Therefore, a new section is formed to emphasize the characteristic of this step. Companies have to make an investment plan before starting the decision making process. This step is a strategic plan for the investment. The critical variable for this section is the product strategy. Appropriate locations differ based on the objectives of the investment and the product strategy. Companies have to consider the products that they want to produce in the location and their future prospects if there may be any changes in the product strategy for a specified location or not. This is especially critical for greenfield operations since it is a concrete investment for a location.

Location Factors Selection

Customized location factors lists are developed in Part V. These lists provide suggestions about the importance levels of the factors based on the sector type, corporate strategy, organizational culture and product strategy of a company. Companies have to understand that different location factors gain importance based on the level of the decision-making. One standard list is not enough for the accurate decision for a specific company. The suggested lists are open to modification considering particular preferences of companies due to their organizational cultures or specific practices.

External Environment Analysis

This section includes the assessment of the candidate countries. An initial list of candidate countries should be available according to company's past experiences in international investments and their internal knowledge. After determining the countries, companies have to find the right data sources to learn more about the countries. Right data sources are critical since the location analysis is going to be all dependent on these data. If the data are incorrect, the decision will be inaccurate. Following are the data sources for international investment decisions.

Data Sources

In the external environment analysis step, companies can reach the right data sources from the following links. Most of them provide generic information about the country and the regulations. If a company wants to get specific data, it has to conduct a detailed data search in that country. In most cases, embassies and/or chamber of commerces are very helpful for a start. This section presents the data sources for country information, country contacts, and US quotas, rules, and regulations.

Country Information

- Country Commercial Guides (CCG)
  http://www.usatrade.gov/website/ccg.nsf/ccghomepage?openform
  Country Commercial Guides (CCG) are prepared by U.S. Embassy Staff once a
year and contain comprehensive information on the business and economic situation of
foreign countries and the political climate as it affects U.S. business. Each CCG covers
topics such as marketing, trade regulations, investment climate and business travel.
Below is the table of contents of a country report.

  1. Executive Summary
  2. Economic Trends And Outlook
  3. Political Environment
  4. Marketing Us Products And Services
  5. Leading Sectors For Us Exports And Investments
  6. Trade Regulations, Customs And Standards
  7. Investment Climate Statement
  8. Trade And Project Financing
  9. Business Travel
  10. Economic And Trade Statistics
  11. Us And Country Contacts
  12. Market Research
  13. Trade Event Schedule

- Background Notes
  http://www.state.gov/r/pa/ei/bgn/

  Background Notes are updated by U.S. Embassy Staff approximately once a year
and contain comprehensive information on the cultural, political, historical, economic
and travel situation of individual foreign countries. Users can search *Background Notes*
by individual country.

- World Factbook (CIA)
  http://www.odci.gov/cia/publications/factbook/

The CIA's *World Factbook* is updated annually by the CIA's country analysts. The *World Factbook* contains many of the same subjects covered by the U.S. State Department's *Background Notes*, including the cultural, political, historical, economic and travel situation of individual foreign countries, but from a much different perspective. This source also provides a much more in-depth factual and statistical background on each country. Users can search *World Factbook* by individual country or by "field listing" (i.e. currencies worldwide, exports by country, etc.).

- US-Mexico Chamber of Commerce
  http://www.usmcoc.org/index2.html

A group of distinguished Mexican and U.S. businessmen established the United States-Mexico Chamber of Commerce (USMCOC) in 1973 as a 501 (c) (6) non-profit business association chartered in Washington D.C. The coalition of businessmen created a bilateral organization to promote trade, investment and joint ventures on both sides of the border.

- IMD World Competitiveness Yearbook
  http://www.imd.ch/wcy
  The World Competitiveness Yearbook analyzes and ranks the ability of nations featuring 49 industrialized and emerging economies (2002)
- Latin Trade
  http://www.latintrade.com/newsite/index.cfm

  This site presents latest news and data about Latin America.

- Country Resources
  http://www.texwatch.com/countryres/index.cfm

There are listed news, profile, company profiles, and industry reports for selected countries.

- CBI Sourcing
  http://www.cbisourcing.com/

This is a website for CBI sourcing. Unifi Inc. is the sponsor for the website. There is a general CBI information section and a database of the US and Caribbean textile companies.

- Country Information
  http://www.ginfo.net/

This website provides very current economic information, site location information, and specific information on subjects including logistics/transportation, economic development sites, international law, and manufacturing.

- Country Risk Rating Website
  http://www.coface-usa.com/

Country Contacts

- The US Embassies
  http://usembassy.state.gov/

This US Department site lists information for embassies located in Washington, DC and will also permit users to access a number of other websites.

- Economic Development Agencies
  http://www.siteselection.com/

- Embassies and Consulates
  http://www.escapeartist.com/embassy1/embassy1.htm

This private source site lists information, addresses and contact personnel to embassies and consulates all over the world.

US Quotas, Rules and Regulations

- US Custom's Electronic Bulletin Board
  http://www.cebb.customs.treas.gov/public/cgi/cebb.exe?mode=fa&area=13

The U.S. Customs Service's *Customs Electronic Bulletin Board* provides Customs' ports and field offices with the latest "Trade Operations Instructions" on how Customs personnel should process U.S. imports.

http://www.cebb.customs.treas.gov/public/cgi/cebb.exe?mode=fa&area=22

Through the *Customs Electronic Bulletin Board*, the U.S. Customs Service provides daily and weekly updates on quota fill rates by country and by apparel/textile category.

- US Custom's Bulletin (weekly)
  http://www.customs.gov/about/bulletin/archives.htm

Updated weekly, the *Customs Bulletin* contains the text of all of the latest Customs rulings and Court of International Trade decisions, many of which affect U.S. imports of apparel and footwear. The Customs rulings are listed in the "General Notices" section of each *Customs Bulletin*.

- Committee for the Implementation of Textile Agreements (CITA)
  http://www.otexa.ita.doc.gov/fr.htm

The Committee for the Implementation of Textile Agreements (CITA) controls all U.S. quota allocations and many other issues concerning U.S. imports of apparel. This Website contains the latest CITA announcements, including changes in individual country quota allocation, application of "short supply" under various trade preference arrangements and numerous other important U.S. apparel import issues.

- National Institute for Standards and Technology
  http://ts.nist.gov/ts/htdocs/210/217/export-alert.htm

By registering for the National Institute for Standards and Technology's (NIST) Export Alert service, U.S. companies receive, via e-mail, notifications of drafts of new or changes to current foreign regulations for a specific industry sector and/or region. Notifications of the proposed foreign regulation contain a description of the regulation, the country issuing the regulation and a final date for comments.

- USA Trade

http://www.usatrade.gov/website/mrd.nsf/SearchMarketResearch

Containing reports written by the commercial staff located in U.S Embassies and Consulates worldwide, this U.S. Department of Commerce Commercial Service Website provides the user with some of the best market research available to U.S. businesses. It is updated daily.

- American Textile Manufacturers Institute (ATMI)
  http://www.atmi.org/EconTradeData/index.asp

ATMI provides a series of reports providing an in-depth review of the U.S. Textile Market from an economic standpoint.

Collection of data is the next step in the external environment analysis. After collecting the data using data sources, companies have to analyze both the qualitative and the quantitative data. This analysis part can be conducted more effectively by using a solution generator due to the vast amount of data and the complexity of analyzing qualitative data.

Solution Generator - Customized Investment Decisions Tool

A solution generator is necessary for international investment decisions due to the complexity of the process. As explained in Part II, this type of decision is a multi-criteria decision and a multi-level decision. Because of these characteristics, an analytical approach is needed to better evaluate vast amount of data. Especially, the use of qualitative data causes difficulties in the decision-making process since this type of data is not inherently metric in nature. Thus, it is hard to consider both the qualitative and the quantitative data in the same calculation and make a decision at the end. However, the decision-maker should consider both types of data simultaneously. Therefore, a solution generator is essential to ease the decision-making process considering the characteristics of international investment decisions.

A decision support tool was developed for international investment decisions using Microsoft Access®. This software was chosen because of the need of a database to store data about candidate countries. The purposes of this decision support tool are:

188

- To generate an effective method to analyze vast data about countries

- To develop a way to quantify the qualitative data

- To develop an all inclusive tool, which can consider both the qualitative and the quantitative parts

- To generate a database for companies to store relevant data for future references

Model Logic

The model logic of the 'Customized Investment Decision Tool' is shown in Figure 33. After the decision-maker enters the program, s/he can choose two ways: to enter/view data to the system or to analyze countries for a specific decision. Before doing the country analysis, enough data should be entered to the system. Therefore, first time users have to choose the data entry part first and enter relevant information about the countries. Country analysis can be performed after this initial step.

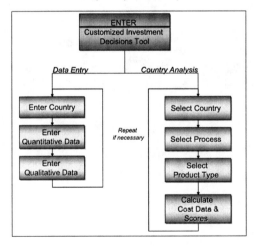

Figure 33 Model logic of the customized investment decision tool

189

Data Entry

A decision-maker can enter new data or view existing data. The key point is, if a new country entry is performed, country name has to be specified as the first step. After entering the country name, data for cost and qualitative factors are entered.

Country Analysis

The decision-maker should select the country to analyze as a first step. Then, the process to be performed in that country has to be selected. In the tool, spinning, knitting/weaving, dyeing/finishing and sewing processes are defined. The required product type should be determined. After these decisions, the related data from the database are called. Cost data and scores for the country are calculated at the end using these data.

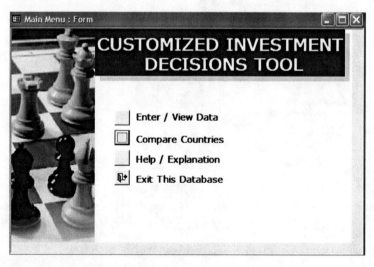

Figure 34 Main menu of the tool

Model Construction

Description of Different Forms

There are three types of forms in the program:

1. General Country Information

2. Cost Data

3. Qualitative Data

General Country Information Form

General country information form (Figure 35) includes the following variables: data about population, languages, official holidays, literacy rate, religion, participation in trade groups, economic data and trade data for textile and apparel industry of the country. This form aims to give summary information about the country at a high level.

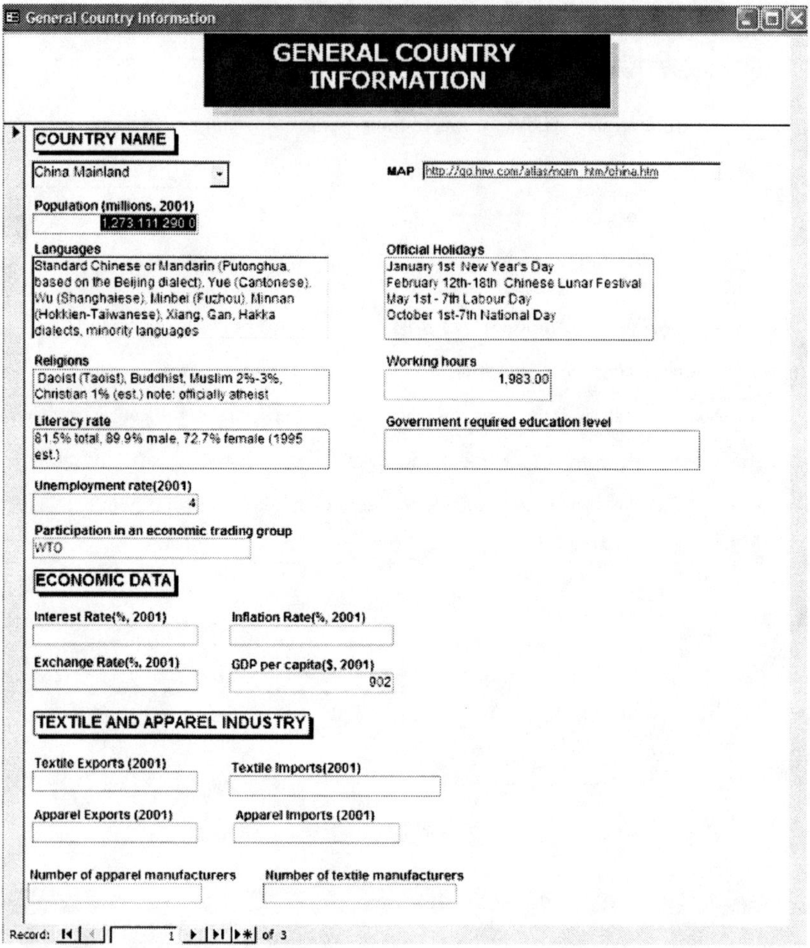

General Country Information

GENERAL COUNTRY INFORMATION

COUNTRY NAME

China Mainland

MAP http://go.hrw.com/atlas/norm_htm/china.htm

Population (millions, 2001)
1,273,111,290.0

Languages
Standard Chinese or Mandarin (Putonghua, based on the Beijing dialect), Yue (Cantonese), Wu (Shanghaiese), Minbei (Fuzhou), Minnan (Hokkien-Taiwanese), Xiang, Gan, Hakka dialects, minority languages

Official Holidays
January 1st New Year's Day
February 12th-18th Chinese Lunar Festival
May 1st - 7th Labour Day
October 1st-7th National Day

Religions
Daoist (Taoist), Buddhist, Muslim 2%-3%, Christian 1% (est.) note: officially atheist

Working hours
1,983.00

Literacy rate
81.5% total, 89.9% male, 72.7% female (1995 est.)

Government required education level

Unemployment rate(2001)
4

Participation in an economic trading group
WTO

ECONOMIC DATA

Interest Rate(%, 2001)

Inflation Rate(%, 2001)

Exchange Rate(%, 2001)

GDP per capita($, 2001)
902

TEXTILE AND APPAREL INDUSTRY

Textile Exports (2001)

Textile Imports(2001)

Apparel Exports (2001)

Apparel Imports (2001)

Number of apparel manufacturers

Number of textile manufacturers

Record: 1 of 3

Figure 35 General country information form

Cost Data Form

Cost data form aims to let user enter the cost data of the country for a specified product. Cost data can be specified up to five different processes. These are:

- Spinning cost data

- Knitting/weaving cost data

- Dyeing/finishing cost data

- Cutting/sewing cost data

- Transportation cost data

Figure 36 An example of a cost data form

Qualitative Data Form

Qualitative data form includes different sections that were analyzed in Part V. Different forms were developed to capture data about the country. Two types of data are collected for these forms: Secondary data and survey data about the country. Secondary data is the quantitative data about the country which can be found from published resources. Survey data, on the other hand, is collected through interviews with the executives from necessary departments in that country. This method is adapted from IMD World Competitiveness Yearbook, 2002 (IMD World Competitiveness Yearbook, 2002).

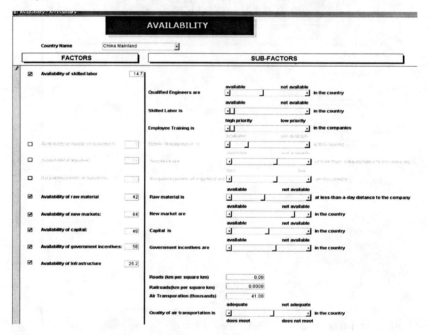

Figure 37 An example of a qualitative data form

Structure of the Model

1. Cost data is calculated through cost forms according to the selected country and product type.

2. Qualitative data is analyzed using different forms for different categories. Figure 38 shows an example of availability category the relationship

194

between the factors and their sub-factors. Each factor is defined, in other words, quantified with the aid of one or more sub-factors. These sub-factors can be published data for countries and survey data that is collected through a series of interviews with the experts in the related country. Survey data is based on a 100 point scale. Published data are also converted to the same scale using the minimum and maximum values of the related data for 49 countries listed in IMD World Competitiveness Yearbook. Then, total scores are calculated for each group by calculating the average of the factors in each group.

3. A summary table presents both the cost data and the scores to provide an overall understanding about the countries and selected processes. Each total score of the seven categories are collected from the related tables and cost figures are collected according to the selected processes from the related tables. Total cost is calculated at the end considering the transportation cost among the countries if processes are handled in different countries

Assumptions

- Each sub-factor has the same rate of effect on the factors. For example, if there are five sub-factors to determine the score of a factor. Average is taken to calculate the score for the factor.
- Each factor has the same rate of effect on the groups.
- Regardless of the product type and the process type, qualitative data for a country remain the same.

FACTOR	SUB-FACTOR	DESCRIPTION
Availability of skilled labor	Qualified Engineers	Qualified engineers are not available in your country's labor market(100), available(1)
	Skilled Labor	Skilled labor is not available in the country's labor market (100), available(1)
	Employee Training	Employee training is a high priority in companies(100), low (1)
Availability of middle management	Availability of middle management	Middle management is available(100), not available(1)
Availability of suppliers	Availability of suppliers	Suppliers are available at less-than-a day distance (100), not available(1)
Bargaining power of suppliers	Bargaining power of suppliers	Bargaining power of suppliers is high(1), low(100)
Availability of raw material	Availability of raw material	Raw Materials are available at less-than-a day distance (100), not available(1)
Availability of new markets	Availability of new markets	New markets are available(100), not available(1)
Availability of capital	Availability of capital	Capital is available(100), not available(1)
Availability of government incentives	Availability of government incentives	Government incentives are available for investment(100), not available(1)
Availability of Infrastructure	Roads	Density of network (km per square km)
	Railroads	Density of network (km per square km)
	Air Transportation	Number of passengers carried by main companies per year
	Quality of air transportation	Quality of air transportation is generally adequate and efficient in your country(100), not adequate(1)
	Water transportation	Water transportation meets business requirements(100), does not meet(1)
	Energy infrastructure	Energy infrastructure is adequate and efficient in your country(100), not adequate(1)
	Fixed telephone lines	Number of main lines per 1000 inhabitants
	New information technology	New information technology and its implementation meet business requirements(100), does not meet(1)
	Internet users	Number of internet users per 1000 people
Quality of the product	Quality of the product	Quality of the product is high (100), low (1) in the defined tolerances
Productivity in industry	Productivity in industry	Estimates: Related GDP(PPP) per person employed in industry, US$
Health, Safety & Env. Concerns	Health, Safety & Env. Concerns	Health, safety & environmental concerns are adequately addressed by management(100), not addressed (1)
Ethical standards	Ethical standards	Ethical practices are very well implemented in companies (100), not implemented (1)

190

Figure 38 Factor-sub-factor relationship for availability category to quantify the qualitative data

Logic of the Strategic Model

The flow of the model is depicted by using arrows in Figure 32. There are four main phases in the model. The first phase starts with recalling the sector that a company operates. A customized list has to be formed considering this sector type. Part V offers this customized list considering four different types of sectors: fiber, textiles, apparel and nonwoven. Determining a list of countries should be performed considering the companies' sector types. This variable was chosen as a first step since it reflects the reason of being for a company. Besides, it has a broader perspective than the rest of the variables. The main idea is to form a broad list of countries and reduced down the list according to the variables specified in the figure at the end of each step. After collecting the data in the external environment analysis section, companies can be evaluated according to the 'Customized Location Factors List according to the Sector Type'. This evaluation can be performed using the 'Customized Investment Decisions Tool'. At the end of the evaluation, some of the countries would be eliminated according to the scores that they got at the end of running the solution generator.

Companies start the second phase with a revised list of countries. At this step, they recall their corporate strategy: cost leadership, differentiation or focus. This time remaining countries are evaluated using a new location factors list. Corporate strategy preference of a company forms the basis of this list. Factors or only the importance levels of factors change as the basis of the step changes. Some of the countries are eliminated at the step considering the new list of factors and their scores based on these factors. The scores are generated using the 'Customized Investment Decisions Tool'.

At the third phase, the same process is repeated however; this time the focus is the organizational culture of the company. Organizational culture for international investments is defined by the risk taking behaviors of the companies. The customized

191

list of location factors according to the organizational culture should be used in the evaluation.

The remaining countries at the end of the third phase should further be evaluated according to a more specific step. A customized list according to the product strategy is used at this phase. Final decision is given after this last evaluation. Remaining countries are analyzed and decision of where to invest is given according to the total scores of the remaining countries.

DISCUSSION & CONCLUSIONS

Textile and apparel companies, everywhere in the world, are considering or are changing their patterns of production due to internationalization and/or globalization. Most of the leading textile and apparel companies in the US have invested in several locations outside of their home country, and most of them have failed to recognize (financially and strategically) full potential of their investments. The fundamental assumption of this study is that these failures were due to some serious flaws in the international investment decision-making process. Companies, most of the time, start the decision-making process with only analyzing generic location factors like labor cost, utilities cost, and trade agreements. However, it is not effective to use the same factors list for all of the companies, regardless of their internal needs, the sector in which they operate, and the values and beliefs of the company. Companies should focus on both the internal and the external environment to be able to make effective international investments.

The need for this extensive decision-making requires a structured decision-making process for international investments. This paper presents a strategic model that considers both:

- o the internal environment of the company by questioning the sector type, strategic approach and the organizational culture of the company, and

198

o the external environment of the company by considering the important location factors.

Several variables are considered to define the above dimensions. Based on the survey and case study results (Part V), several of these variables were found to have no direct effect on the international investment decisions. After the elimination of these variables a strategic model is developed considering the remaining variables, which were: corporate strategy and product strategy in the strategy dimension, risk taking behavior in the organizational culture and the sector type. These variables were incorporated to the five-section model.

All of the variables, mentioned above, represent the internal environment of the company. Based on the survey results it was found that these variables were not important for the decision making process at the same time. There are different steps in the country selection process. For example, the corporate strategy variable is important in a higher level in the decision making process than the product strategy. Companies first try to decide the list of countries based on their corporate strategies, and then they narrow down this list considering their product strategy. This finding from the case study results provided the backbone for this strategic model.

There are five sections and four steps in the strategic model. Five sections are:

- Internal Environment Analysis
- International Investment Plan
- Location Factors Selection
- External Environment Analysis
- Solution Generator

Internal environment provides a clear understanding of the company's needs and its objectives. Sector type, corporate strategy and organizational culture are the variables for this section.

199

International investment plan, on the other hand, is specific to the investment decision. It introduces the specific investments' objectives and strategies. Product strategy is the variable for this section.

In the location factors selection, customized lists for each variable is presented. These lists were formed based on the survey and case study results in Part V.

External environment analysis is the step where companies find candidate countries and analyze their performance considering the factors in the related customized location factors list. Solution generator is a decision support tool that helps analyze countries more effectively.

Four steps in the model are the variables that have effects on the international investment decisions:

- Sector Type
- Corporate Strategy
- Organizational Culture
- Product Strategy

The model starts with the first variable, sector type. A customized location factors list according to the sector type is considered and countries are analyzed using the solution generator. Based on the total scores of the countries that are generated by the solution generator, some of the countries are eliminated and the second step begins with this reduced list. The same process continues for the rest of the variables and decision can be reached at the end of the fourth step. Thus, the solution generator provides valuable contribution by providing a way for decision-makers to quantify the qualitative data.

In conclusion, this all-inclusive model presents a structured way of decision-making for international investment decisions by allowing the decision-maker ease in the complexity of the multi-level and multi-criteria decision-making process.

Future work may include a sensitivity analysis using the developed model and the decision support tool. The weightings or the values of the location factors can be changed and their effect on the result can be analyzed. In addition, probabilistic distributions can be used to reflect the effects of the decision-maker's preferences.

Different methodologies like simulation can be used as a decision support tool to enhance the consideration of the uncertainty in the environment since these methodologies are more capable of reflecting the risk/uncertainty as discussed in Part II.

REFERENCES

Bartmess, A. D., & Cerny, K. (1993). Building Competitive Advantage through a Global Network of Capabilities. California Management Review(Winter), 78-103.

Brush, T. H., Maritan, C. A., & Karnani, A. (1999). The Plant Location Decision in Multinational Manufacturing Firms:An Empirical Analysis of International Business and Manufacturing Strategy Perspectives. Production and Operations Management, 8(2), 109-132.

Notes on Facility Location. (1989). Harvard Business College

Govindarajan, V., & Gupta, A. K. (2001). The Quest for Global Dominance. San Francisco, CA: Jossey-Bass.

Heisler, E. (2003, March 16, 2003). Struggle:South of the border; the textile experiment in Mexico showed promise, but problems piled up quickly. Ultimately, corporate mistakes and economic misfortuns led to failures. The News & Record.

IMD World Competitiveness Yearbook. (2002). IMD International.

Kotler, P. (2003). Marketing Management (11th ed.). New Jersey: Prentice Hall.

MacCormack, A. D., Newman, L. J. I., & Rosenfield, D. B. (1994). The New Dynamics of Global Manufacturing Site Location. Sloan Management Review(Summer), 69-80.

Schmenner, R. W. (1979). Look Beyond the Obvious in Plant Location. Harvard Business Review(January-February), 126-132.

Vos, B. (1997). Redesigning International Manufacturing and Logistics Structures. International Journal of Physical Distribution & Logistics Management, 27(7), 377-394.

PART VII: CONCLUSIONS AND RECOMMENDATIONS

SUMMARY AND CONCLUSIONS

Companies often try to exploit their competitive advantage by using the comparative advantage of geographical differences. However, this process requires a tremendous amount of effort and capital. In addition, there always exists the possibility of ultimate failure due to long term and short term uncertainty in the environment. Many American companies fail to realize the full potential of their foreign investments and Hoch (1982) argues that faulty location selection is the major cause for this shortfall.

Today, the failure of investment decisions has contributed to the struggle that US textile and apparel companies have faced. Patterns of global production and trade have changed after several major agreements for the US Textile and Apparel industry. The decision to manufacture in the US is always considered, in terms of it being the right decision or not. The failures in Mexico showed that there was something wrong in the decision-making process of those companies. They did not analyze the decisions thoroughly and overlooked some parts. However, it is also clear that staying in the US is not the right solution for all types of the textile companies. The discussion of finding the right investment revealed the need for an investigation about international investment decisions.

After reviewing the literature (Parts II, III), in this research

- Different methodologies for decision-making were analyzed for the textile and apparel industry considering the multi-criteria, multi-period and multilevel characteristics of the international investment decisions. The methods like scaling, scoring, ranking were found to be user-friendly and easy to develop however, the models that can incorporate uncertainty, like mathematical programming, heuristic algorithms and simulation appeared as more appropriate methodologies for the textile and apparel industry when uncertainty and risk in the environment were concerned (Part II).

- A new list of location factors were developed according to the needs of the today's environment (Part III).

- A comprehensive instrument for customized investment decisions was developed considering the strategy of the company, the organizational culture of the company, the sector where the company operates, and the role of external environment. This instrument can serve as a comprehensive tool since it covers the important dimensions for a company and as an effective tool since it provides customization for different needs of companies (Part IV).

- An empirical study was conducted within the textile and apparel industry. According to the results of this study, textile and apparel companies were not using a structured decision-making process. A combination of customer/market researches and scenario analysis were mentioned by some of the companies in the study as a tool for the international investment decisions (Part V).

- To develop this structured decision-making process, the importance of the location factors were asked to textile and apparel companies using survey and case study methods. Results were analyzed according to the strategy, organizational culture and the sector of the company dimensions. The following variables appeared to have an effect on international investment decisions: corporate strategy and product strategy for the strategy dimension; the risk taking behavior for the organizational culture dimension and fiber, textile, apparel and nonwovens for the sector type dimension (Part V).

- Growth strategy and operational strategy variables for strategy dimension had reflected no effect on the ratings of the location factors. However, the effect of the growth strategy was expected due to the different concentrations of a greenfield operation investor from a sourcing investor (Part V).

- Using the survey results, a categorization was conducted within each found-to-be-effective variable: corporate strategy, product strategy, risk taking behavior

205

and the sector type. This categorization reflected the importance levels of the factors as: must factors, highly recommended factors and optional factors, for each variable (Part V).

- Based on a case study, it was found that the multilevel characteristic of the international investment decisions (country selection, region selection and site selection) was even valid for the county selection level. Each variable (e.g., corporate strategy, sector type) is considered at the different phases of the decision-making for the country selection. This result was, then, used as a basis for the strategic model that was presented in Part VI.

- A strategic model was developed considering the results of the empirical studies for the textile and apparel industry. The backbone of the model was constructed according to the variables which were found effective in international investment decisions. Then, a four phase model is developed with a sequence of conducting internal environment analysis, developing a customized location factors list, collecting the relevant data using the data sources and analyzing the data with the solution generator. This model is an all-inclusive model with a consideration of the internal and the external environment of the company (Part VI).

- A listing of relevant data sources were gathered for the textile and apparel industry (Part VI).

- A new interpretation was developed using the IMD World Competitiveness Yearbook (2002). Appropriate sub-factors were selected form their list of factors to quantify the qualitative data in the decision support tool. The same method was applied for the factors that were not available in their list.

CONTRIBUTIONS

Specific contributions to the following areas are discussed in this section:

- Literature

- Methodology

- Model Development

- The Textile and Apparel Industry

Contributions to Literature

In Part II, different methodologies offering different decision-making techniques were analyzed for plant location selection. Models, mainly based on the decision maker's preferences (e.g., scaling, scoring, ranking, AHP), traditional mathematical programming models, latest solution methodologies (e.g. heuristic algorithms and simulation) were examined. Overall, all of the methodologies, explained in Part II, have advantages and disadvantages when international plant location decisions are concerned. Decision makers should select the right solution for the needs of their company and the current market dynamics. After a detailed analysis for each methodology, the advantages and disadvantages of the methodologies for international plant location were summarized as a contribution to the literature.

In Part III, a list of 49 factors was developed with the aid of the literature survey, the interviews with companies, the experience of the university professors and the consulting experience of the author. Seven categories: cost, availability, accessibility, quality, risk/uncertainty, ease of operations, and quality of life are formed to categorize these factors. This comprehensive list, as a contribution to literature, was formed according to today's needs after analyzing the environment from different perspectives, and this list was then used as the foundation of a decision-making tool for international investments.

In Part VI, the literature for international investments, which focused on different business environments of the company, were discussed. The contribution of the model in Part VI was to the part of the literature that considered both the internal and the external environment of the company.

Contributions to Methodology

In Part IV, the traditional investment decision-making process was questioned and a new instrument was introduced, one which also offers a basis for a new methodology for international investment decisions. The traditional decision-making process, including three steps of determining the candidate countries, analyzing these countries based on a generic location factors list, and making the final decision was discussed as it embodies serious flaws for today's environment. The new methodology includes the need for an additional step, customization was addressed due to companies' specific needs.

A comprehensive instrument for customized investment decisions with a modification of the traditional decision-making process is presented in Part IV with an additional step of customization of the location factors. This customization is conducted according to the strategy of the company, the organizational culture of the company, the sector where the company operates, and the role of external environment. "Customized Investment Decisions Instrument" was developed to guide the companies to an effective customization of the location factors and their priorities according to the companies' needs.

In Part V, survey and case study methodologies were used as the data collection strategy for understanding the decision-making process of textile and apparel companies for international investment decisions. The results support the continued use of a combined data collection approach when working with proprietary sensitive topics.

In Part VI, an interpretation was developed to quantify the qualitative location factors in the "Customized Investment Decisions Instrument". Using the IMD World Competitiveness Yearbook (2002), a table of the factors and the sub-factors are presented in Part VI. Interpretation of qualitative factors with some quantitative data is not a new method, however selection of the appropriate quantitative data for use as representation for the qualitative data is new. Thus, this part contributes the methodology of quantifying the qualitative data that should be included as part of the international investment decisions process.

Contributions to Model Development

In Part VI, a strategic model was developed that considers both:

- o the internal environment of the company by questioning the sector type, strategic approach and the organizational culture of the company, and
- o the external environment of the company by considering the important location factors.

As a contribution to model development, this all-inclusive model presents a structured way of decision-making for international investment decisions.

Contributions to the Textile and Apparel Industry

In Part II, the survey of different methodologies for plant location decisions was conducted. The suitability of these methods to the textile and apparel industry was discussed. In today's environment, uncertainty or risk incorporation is the most critical concern for textile and apparel industries. With the elimination of tariffs and quotas in 2005 and several trade agreements such as NAFTA and CBI, textile and apparel companies are forced to do business in such a volatile environment. In this respect,

209

scaling/scoring/ranking methods and AHP are easy to develop and use but they are incompetent in reflecting a good snapshot for the future, especially, when uncertainty and risk in the environment are concerned. For textile and apparel industries, especially for textile industry, a more accurate prediction of the future is critical since the level of investment is really high. Then, the models that can incorporate uncertainty, like mathematical programming, heuristic algorithms and simulation appear as the appropriate methodologies. In addition, developing realistic models using mathematical programming is limited because of the strict assumptions such as linearity. If companies may release the need for an accurate solution, heuristics and simulation would remain as the most appropriate methods for textile and apparel industry.

Prior to the research in Part V, no instrument existed that was specifically for the textile and apparel industry. The 'Customized Investment Decisions Tool' was used as the instrument of the survey and case studies modified and tested with the textile industry. The tool consists of 49 location factors divided into seven categories. The categories are: cost, availability, accessibility, quality, risk/uncertainty, ease of operations and quality of life.

RECOMMENDATIONS FOR FUTURE WORK

In Part III, a new list of location factors is presented. This list was mainly formed with the aid of the literature review. Interviews were conducted, however, they were not enough to prove that this list represents the important factors for the textile and apparel industry. A list, specific to the textile and apparel industry, can be formed by detailed case studies that can be conducted with textile and apparel companies. Most of the time the factors might be the same however, their interpretation or sub-factors might be different.

In Part IV, it is believed that it will be useful if future work can be an implementation of this instrument to different sectors, to model the decision-making behaviors. Another suggestion would be to update the dimensions according to the changing dynamics of the environment. Today the most important and comprehensive dimensions are strategy, culture, sectors type and external environment. However, new dimensions may emerge in the future that should be considered or the definitions of the used dimensions may change and it may be necessary to update the instrument accordingly in the future. Besides, some of the factors in the location factors list can measure the same factor. So, if statistically significant survey data can be collected, it is recommended to conduct factor analysis with the location factors list (Part III).

During the case study interviews, a new dimension was appeared to represent the internal environment of the companies. This dimension is the ownership of the company: whether it is a public company or a private company. It can be examined using the tools in this research.

In Part V, survey and case studies were used as the research methodology. There appeared limitations for the survey implementation. If future research aims to implement surveys, the disadvantages mentioned in Part V have to be considered. Surveys are appropriate for collection of extensive amount of data; however, in this case the data sought were proprietary. If this barrier to obtaining data disappears in future, surveys are suggested as data collection methodology. However, if this continues to be a burden in the future, extensive case studies are suggested for future research.

In Part II, different methodologies are presented and scaling method is selected as a solution generator in Part VI. Other methodologies for greenfield operations (plant location decisions) can be used in a combined fashion since limitations of the methodologies might be diminished by using a combined method. Future research may analyze the combinations of these different methodologies to reach a better solution for international investment decisions.

211

The strategic model in Part VI was developed according to a single sector type. The model can be modified to serve the needs of a vertically integrated company as a future research.

The strategic model can be applied to the companies in the textile and apparel industry. The results can be analyzed to validate the model. On the other hand, companies can use the model for their own needs, besides government agencies can conduct surveys and analyze the results to find out in which factor to invest to attract the investment to their specific state.

COMPREHENSIVE REFERENCE LIST

Andrews, D. C. (1995). Can organizational culture be reengineered? Enterprise Reengineering, Oct/Nov(http://www.c3i.osd.mil/bpr/bprcd/5304.htm).

Badri, M. A. (1999). Combining the Analytic Hierarchy Process and Goal Programming for Global Facility Location-Allocation Problem. International Journal of Production Economics, 62, 237-248.

Badri, M. A., Davis, D. L., & Davis, D. (1995). Decision Support Models for the Location of Firms in Industrial Sites. International Journal of Operations & Production Management, 15(1), 50-62.

Bair, J., & Gereffi, G. (2002). NAFTA and the apparel commodity chain: Corporate strategies, interfirm networks, and industrial upgrading. In J. Bair (Ed.), Free Trade and Uneven Development (pp. 356). Philadelphia: Temple University Press.

Ballou, R. H. (1968). Dynamic Warehouse Location Analysis. Journal of Marketing Research, 7, 271-276.

Bartmess, A. D., & Cerny, K. (1993). Building Competitive Advantage through a Global Network of Capabilities. California Management Review(Winter), 78-103.

Bauer, R. J., Jr. (1994). Genetic Algorithms and Investment Strategies. New York: John Wiley & Sons, Inc.

Benjamin, C. O., Chi, S., Gaber, T., & Riordan, C. A. (1995). Comparing BP and ART II Neural Network Classifiers for Facility Location. Computers and Industrial Engineering, 28(1), 43-50.

Birnbaum, D. (2000). Birnbaum's Global Guide to Winning the Great Garment War. Hong Kong: Third Horizon Press Limited.

Brimberg, J., & ReVelle, C. (1999). A multi-facility location model with partial satisfaction of demand. Studies in Locational Analysis, 13, 91-101.

Brimberg, J., & ReVelle, C. (2000). The maximum return-on-investment plant location. Journal of the Operational Research Society, 51, 729-735.

Brush, T. H., Maritan, C. A., & Karnani, A. (1999). The Plant Location Decision in Multinational Manufacturing Firms: An Emprical Analysis of International Business and Manufacturing Strategy Perspectives. Production and Operations Management, 8(2), 109-132.

Burritt, C. (2000, Dec 17, 2000). Seven years into NAFTA, textile makers seek payoff in Mexico\Textiles: Payoff Sought in Mexico. The Atlanta Journal-Constitution.

Camuffo, A., Romano, P., & Vinelli, A. (2001). Back to the future: Benetton transforms its global network. MIT Sloan Management Review(Fall), 46-52.

Canel, C., & Das, S., R. (2002). Modeling Global Facility Location Decisions: Integrating Marketing and Manufacturing Decisions. Industrial Management & Data Systems, 102(2), 110-118.

Canel, C., & Khumawala, B. M. (1997). Multi-period international facilities location: An algorithm and application. International Journal of Production Research, 35(7), 1891-1910.

Chakravarty, A. K. (1999). Profit margin, process improvement and capacity decisions in global manufacturing. International Journal of Production Research, 37(18), 4235-4257.

Chuang, P. T. (2001). Combining the Analytical Hierarchy Process and Quality Function Deployment for a Location Decision from a Requirement Perspective. The International Journal of Advanced Manufacturing Technology, 18, 842-849.

Cox, T. J. (1993). Cultural Diversity in Organizations: Theory, Research & Practice. San Francisco: Berett-Koehler.

Current, J., Ratick, S., & ReVelle, C. (1997). Dynamic Facility Location When the Total Number of Facilities is Uncertain: A Decision Analysis Approach. European Journal of Operational Research, 110, 597-609.

Dickerson, K. (1999). Textiles and apparel in the global economy. New Jersey: Prentice-Hall, Inc.

Dillman, D. A. (2000). Mail and Internet Surveys: The Tailored Design Method (second ed.). Canada: John Wiley & Sons Inc.

Dunning, J. H. (1988). The Eclectic Paradigm of International Production: A Restatement and Some Possible Extensions. Journal of International Business Studies(Spring), 1-31.

Govindarajan, V., & Gupta, A. K. (2001). The Quest for Global Dominance. San Francisco, CA: Jossey-Bass.

Hax, A., & Majluf, S. (1983). The Industry Attractiveness-Business Strength Matrix in Strategic Planning. Interfaces, 13(April), 54-71.

Hayter, R. (1997). The Dynamics of Industrial Location: The Factory, The Firm, The Production System. England: John Wiley & Sons.

Heisler, E. (2003, March 16, 2003). Struggle: South of the border; the textile experiment in Mexico showed promise, but problems piled up quickly. Ultimately, corporate mistakes and economic misfortunes led to failures. The News & Record.

Henisz, W., & Delios, A. (2001). Uncertainty, Imitation and Plant Location:Japanese multinational corporations, 1990-1996. Administrative Science Quarterly, 46, 443-475.

Higgins, J. M., & Vincze, J. W. (1993). Strategic Management: Text and Cases (Fifth ed.): The Dryden Press.

Hoch, L. C. (1982). Site Selection for Foreign Operations. Industrial Development, 151, 7-9.

Hoffman, J. J., & Schniederjans, M. J. (1994). A Two-stage Model for Structuring Global Facility Site Selection Decisions. International Journal of Operations & Production Management, 14(4), 79-96.

Holmberg, K., Ronnqvist, M., & Yuan, D. (1999). An Exact Algorithm for the Capacitated Facility Location Problems with Single Sourcing. European Journal of Operational Research, 113(3), 544-559.

Houshyar, A., & White, B. (1997). Comparison of Solution Procedures to the Facility Location Problem. Computers and Industrial Engineering, 32(1), 77-87.

Hunt, J. R., & Koulamas, C. P. (1989). A Model for Evaluating Potential Facility Locations on a Global Basis. SAM Advanced Management Journal(Summer), 19-23.

Ietto_gillies, G. (2000). What role for Multinationals in the New Theories of International Trade and Location? International Review of Applied Economics, 14(4), 413-426.

IMD World Competitiveness Yearbook. (2002). IMD International.

Isard, W. (1956). Location and Space-Economy. New York: The MIT Press.

Joines, J. A. (2002). TE589D Evolutionary Optimization Class Notes.

Kelton, W. D., Sadowski, R. P., & Sadowski, D. A. (2002). Simulation with Arena (Second edition ed.): Mc Graw Hill.

Klincewicz, J. G. (1985). A large-scale Distribution and Location Model. AT&T Technical Journal, 64, 1705-1730.

Kotler, P. (2003). Marketing Management (11th ed.). New Jersey: Prentice Hall.

Kratice, J., Tosic, D., Filipovic, V., & Ljubic, I. (2001). Solving the simple plant location problem by genetic algorithm. RAIRO Operations Research, 35, 127-142.

Law, A. M., & Kelton, W. D. (2000). Simulation Modeling and Analysis (Third Edition ed.): Mc Graw Hill.

Lim, S. K., & Kim, Y. D. (1999). An Integrated Approach to Dynamic Plant Loation and Capacity Planning. Journal of the Operational Research Society, 50, 1205-1216.

MacCarty, B., & Atthirawong, W. (2001). Critical Factors in International Location Decisions: A Delphi study. Paper presented at the Twelfth Annual Conference of the Production and Operations Management Society, Orlando, FL.

MacCormack, A. D., Newman, L. J. I., & Rosenfield, D. B. (1994). The New Dynamics of Global Manufacturing Site Location. Sloan Management Review(Summer), 69-80.

Manne, A. S. (1961). Capacity Extension and Probabilistic Growth. Econometrica, 29, 632649.

Manne, A. S. (1967). Investments for Capacity Expansion:Size, Location, and Time Phasing. Cambridge, MA: MIT Press.

McDonald, A. L. (1986). Of Floating Factories and Mating Dinosaurs. Harvard Business Review, 64(6), 82-86.

McPherson, E. M. (1995). Plant Location Selection Techniques. New Jersey: Noyes Publications.

Murray, J. Y., & Kotabe, M. (1999). Sourcing strategies of US Service companies: A modified transaction cost analysis. Strategic Management Journal, 20, 791-809.

Owen, S. H., & Daskin, M. S. (1998). Strategic Facility Location: A Review. European Journal of Operational Research, 111, 423-447.

Plastria, F. (2001). Static Competitive Facility Location: An Overview of optimization Approaches. European Journal of Operational Research, 129, 461-470.

Porter, M. (1980). Competitive Strategy Techniques for analyzing industries and competitors. New York: The Free Press.

Porter, M. (1990). The Competitive Advantage of Nations. New York: The Free Press.

Porter, M. (1998). Competing Across Locations: Enhancing Competitive Advantage through Global Strategy: Harvard Business School Press.

ReVelle, C., & Laporte, G. (1996). The Plant Location Problem: New Models and Research Prospects. OR Chronicle, 44(6), 864-874.

Ronnqvist, M. (1999). A repeated Matching Heuristic for the Single Source Capacitated Facility Location Problem. European Journal of Operational Research, 116(1), 51-68.

Saaty, T. L. (1988). Multicriteria Decision Making: The Analytic Hierarchy Process. United States.

Saaty, T. L. (1994). Highlights and Critical Points in the Theory and Application of the Analytic Hiearchy Process. European Journal of Operational Research, 74, 426-447.

Schmenner, R. W. (1979). Look Beyond the Obvious in Plant Location. Harvard Business Review(January-February), 126-132.

216

Schmenner, R. W. (1982). Making Business Location Decisions: Prentice-Hall.

Schmidt, G., & Wilhelm, W. E. (2000). Strategic, tactical and operational decisions in multi-national logistics networks:a review and discussion of modelling issues. International Journal of Production Research, 38(7), 1501-1523.

Schniederjans, M. J. (1999). International Facility Acquisition and Location Analysis. London: Quorum Books.

Schniederjans, M. J., & Garvin, T. (1997). Using Analytic Hierarchy Process and Multi-objective Programming for the Selection of Cost Drivers in Activity-based Costing. European Journal of Operational Research, 100, 72-80.

Smith, D. M. (1981). Industrial Location: An economic geographical analysis (second edition ed.). New York: John Wiley&Sons, Inc.

Tombak, M. M. (1995). Multinational Plant Location as a Game of Timing. European Journal of Operational Research, 86, 434-451.

Tong, H.-M. (1979). Plant Location Decision of Foreign Manufacturing Investors. Michigan: UMI Research Press.

Ulgado, F. M. (1996). Location Characteristics of Manufacturing Investments in the US: A Comparison of American and Foreign-based Firms. Management International Review, 36(1), 7-24.

Uncu, S., Hodge, G. L., Oxenham, W., & Jones, M. R. (2002). An Analysis of Current Methodologies for International Plant Location Decisions. Paper presented at the IIFFTI, Hong Kong Polytechnic University, Hong Kong.

Van Weele, A. J., & Rozemeijer, F. A. Revolution in purchasing:Building competitive power through pro-active purchasing. Eindhoven: Technical University.

Verra, G. J. (1999). Global Sourcing: An international survey among multinationals. Paper presented at the Nyenrode Research Papers Series.

Verter, V., & Dasci, A. (2002). The plant location and flexible technology acquisition problem. European Journal of Operational Research, 136, 366-382.

Vos, B. (1997). Redesigning International Manufacturing and Logistics Structures. International Journal of Physical Distribution & Logistics Management, 27(7), 377-394.

Watts, H. (1987). Industrial Geography. New York: Wiley.

Weber, A. (1929). Theory of the Location of Industries. New York: Russell&Russell.

Yang, J., & Lee, H. (1997). An AHP Decision Model for Facility Location Selection. Facilities, 15(9/10 (September/October)), 241-254.

Yurimoto, S., & Masui, T. (1995). Design of a decision support system for overseas plant location in the EC. International Journal of Production Economics, 41, 411-418.

Zahedi, F. (1986). The Analytic Hierarchy Process- A Survey of the Method and its Applications. Interfaces, 16(4(July-August)), 96-108.

APPENDIX A: List of Location Factors According to the Historical Periods

Tong (1979)
Nearness to markets within the US
Proximity to export markets
Nearness to home operations
Nearness to operations in a third country
Facilities of import and export
Proximity to raw material sources
Proximity to suppliers
Availability of managerial and technical personnel
Availability of skilled labor
Availability of unskilled labor
Salary and wage rate
Labor attitudes
Labor laws
Availability of utilities
Cost of utilities
Availability of transportation facilities
Cost of transportation facilities
Availability of suitable plant sites
Cost of suitable land
Cost of construction
Ample space for future expansion
Availability of local capital fund
Cost of local capital fund
State tax rates
Local tax rates
Government incentives
Attutudes of government officials
Attitudes of local citizens
Housing facilities
Education facilities
Police and fire protection

Figure 39 Location factors during Fordist Mass Production (1930s-1980s) Period

Schmenner (1982)	Joint Economic Congress (US) Survey (1982)	Hax and Majluf (1983)
Labor costs	Labor skills/availability	Economic factors
Labor unionization	Labor costs	Technological factors
Transportation costs	Tax climate	Governmental factors
Proximity to raw materials	Academic institutions	Social factors
Proximity to existing company facilities	Cost of living	Industry factors
Quality of life	Transportation	
	Access to markets	
	Regional regulatory practices	
	Energy cost/availability	
	Cultural amenities	
	Climate	
	Access to raw materials	

Office of Technology Assesment (1984)	Christy and Ironside's Alberta Survey (1987)	Watts (1987)
Founding entrepreneurs lived there	Overall business climate	Labor factors
Close to existing operations	Founding entreprenuer lived there	Accesibility factors
Labor skills/availability	Access to markets	Community factors
State government support	Labor skills/availability	Business climate factors
Local transportation	Political stability	Utility factors
Quality of life	Proximity to universities	Plant site factors
High technology business climate	Local government incentives	Financial and special factors
Universities	Proximity to international airport	
Availability of suitable sites	Proximity to domestic airports	
Overall business climate	Provincial government support programme	
Financial incentives	Availability of venture capital	
Venture capital available	Recretional opportunities	
	Local transportatin	
	Access to raw materials	
	Energy costs/ availability	
	Cost of living	
	Cultural amenities	
	Labor costs	
	Proximity to government departments	
	Climate	

Figure 40 Location factors during Information & Communication (1980s-1990s) Period

Bathelt and Hecht's Ontario Survey (1990)	Malecki and Bradbury (1992)	Badri, Davis & Davis (1994)	Yurimoto, Masui (1995)
Availability of skilled labor	Recreational opportunities	Availability of pipeline facilities	Labour
education/birth/residence of the founder	Proximity to major airports	Cost of raw materials & Transportation	Markets
Proximity to universities	Community business attitudes	Availability of unskilled labor	Transportation
Proximity to customer	Restaurants and shopping	None existence of unions	Financial inducement
Access to transportation networks	Environmental quality	Cost of living	Living conditions
Land availability	Overall business climate	Availability of raw materials	
Wage levels	Accessibility to headquarters	Closeness to raw materials	
Proximity to suppliers	Economic growth potential	Location of suppliers	
Land cost	Climate	Freight costs	
Socio/cultural quality	Proximity to universities	Proximity to consumer markets	
	Cultural amenities	Availability of marketing services	
	Cost of housing	Location of competitors	
	Quality of private schools	Size of markets	
	Cost of living	Cost of industrial land	
	Availability of professionals	Cost of developed industrial park	
	Quality of public education	Adequacy of water supply	
	Accesibility to suppliers	Adequacy of sewage facilities	
	Accesibility to markets	Insurance rates	
	Alternative employers for spouse	Safety inspections	
	Traffic congestion	Air pollution	
	Entrepreneurial opportunities	Availability of colleges	
	Proximity to other research facilities	Availability of library facilities	
	Alternative employers for employee	Availability of medical facilities	
	Proximity to similar firms	Availability of banks and credit institutions	
	Nearness to family	Community position of future expansion	

Vos (1996)	Ulgado (1996)	Hayter (1997)	Brush, Maritan & Karnam (1999)
Supply of materials	Local and labor attitudes	Transportation facilities	Proximity to import markets
Labor	Community environment	Materials	Proximity to key customers
Capital	Incentives	Markets	Proximity to key suppliers
Energy	Land and transportation services	Labor	Proximity to other facilities
Distribution	International concerns	External economies	Access to Raw materials
Technology intensity	Synergy logistics	Energy	Access to enery
Control intensity	Input logistics	Community Infrastructure	Access to capital
Labor/capital ratio	Capital concerns	Capital	Access to local technology
Value density	Market logistics	Land/Buildings	Access to skilled labor
	Skilled HR availability	Environment	Access to low cost labor
	Tax rates		Access to protected markets
			Tax conditions
			Regional trade barriers
			Government subsidies
			Exchange rate risk
			Language, culture, politics
			Advanced infrastructure
			Labor practices & regulations
			Environmental regulations

Figure 41 Location factors during Globalization (1990s-2000) Period

MacCarthy & Atthirawang (2001)	Industry week.com (2001)
Favorable labor climate	Labor costs and quality
Transportation costs	Proximity to customers
Proximity to markets and customers	Government incentives
Proximity to suppliers and resources	Transportation infrastructure
Proximity to parent company's facilities	Regulatory/Business climate
Location of competitors	
Quality of environment	
Political factors	
Tax structure related factors	
Social factors	
Economic related factors	
Other related factors	

Figure 42 Location factors during Globalization (2000-present) Period

APPENDIX B: Survey Instrument

International Plant Location Survey

http://www4.ncsu.edu/~suncu/survey/

Thank you for helping with this survey on the ways in which companies make international plant location decisions. Please complete the survey even if you do not have plants outside the US. Our sample consist of companies that may have:

An international plant/plants outside the US

Any kind of strategic partnership with a plant/plants outside the US

No plants outside the states but have gone through the decision making

of locating a plant globally

Your expertise will help us to model the decision making characteristics of different firms precisely. You are a part of a carefully selected sample that has been asked to assist with this survey, and we appreciate your assistance. Your responses will be confidential.

Should you have any difficulties in responding please e-mail us at: suncu@tx.ncsu.edu or call (919) 515-6449.

Thank you for your participation

I. Investment Decisions

Q1. Which of the following plant location experiences did you/your

company go through? (Select all that apply)

Experience :A plant location selection process

Result: An international location

Experience :A plant location selection process with a global

concentration

223

Result : A US location

Experience :A strategic partnership selection process with a global concentration

Result: An international partner

Experience :A strategic partnership selection process with a global concentration

Result: A US partner

Q2.   Which one of the following strategic objectives drives the majority of your company's plant location decisions ? (Check only one of the following choices)

Marketing Strategies (i.e. following your customer, increasing capacity to meet demand, and participating in attractive markets)

Cost Strategies (i.e. reducing total cost of production, and avoidance of tariffs)

Other (Please specify)

Q3.   How important are each one of the following types of international investments for your company?

Building a plant outside the US --click to select-- Very important / Important/ Somewhat important/ Unimportant

Building a strategic partnership with another company outside the US --click to select-- Very important /Important /Somewhat important/ Unimportant

Sourcing from a company outside the US --click to select-- Very important /Important /Somewhat important/ Unimportant

II. Corporate Strategy

Q4.Which one of the following strategies best describes your company's

224

corporate strategy?

Cost Leadership- Aggressive construction of efficient scale facilities, vigorous pursuit of cost reductions

Differentiation- the development of a design or brand image, technology, customer service, which is perceived as unique

Focus- Serving a particular(niche) market very well with a narrow scope

Q5.   How often does your company review its strategy?   --click to select-- Constantly /Every six months/ Every year/ Every two years

Q6.   Which of the following/s describes your company's specific practices? (Select all that apply)

Innovation /   Quality /   Continuous Improvement/   Speed /

Flexibility/   Other

Q7.   Which quality evaluation techniques do your company use?(Select all that apply)

Statistical Process Control(SPC)/ Total Quality Management(TQM)/

Six Sigma Other (please specify)

Q8.   Which techniques do the firm use for plant location decisions? (Select all that apply)

Customer/Market Research Decision Trees

Delphi Method Scenario Analysis

Analytic Hierarchy Process Mathematical Programming

Genetic Algorithms Simulation

Other (please, specify)

Q9.   Thinking about your company's recent plant location decision, how effective are your company's techniques?   --click to select-- not

effective /somewhat effective /effective /very effective

III. Organizational Approach

Please recall your company's last offshore plant location decision , and

answer questions 10-12 based on that project.

If your company operates only in the US , please recall a recent project which

is as critical as plant location projects.

Project (Please specify)

Q10.   Who gave the final decision about the final location ?

                --click to select-- Project group and CEO/ CEO /CEO and

        board members/ All of the above

Q11.   What was the contribution of the project report to the final

        decision ?   --click to select-- None Only slightly contributed

        Somewhat contributed Very much contributed

Q12.   Was there a specific organizatonal value, belief and/or

        principle that affected the decision? Yes   No

        If Yes, please specify

Q13.   How do you define your organization in terms of risk

        taking?   My organization can take --click to select-- High

        risks /Medium risks /Few risks /No risks at all

Q14.   What is the nature of the feedback received from the

        managers? --click to select—constant/ intermittent /at job completion /never

Q15.   What information is shared in the organization?   Needed

        Information /   Desired Information

Q16. On a scale from one to four, with "4" being very important and "1" being

unimportant, please indicate the importance of the following statistics in your company's international plant location decision.

Import and Export Statistics

Annual Growth

GNP

Currency

Foreign Direct Investment(FDI)

Inflation

Other Economic Indicators

Other Economic Indicators

Other Economic Indicators

Other Economic Indicators

Please recall your company's most important product/product line and answer questions 17-18 based on this product/product line.

Product/Product Line(Please specify):

Q17.Which one of the following categories best describes the selected product/product line?

High profit generation / High manufacturing(sourcing) risk

High profit generation / Low manufacturing(sourcing) risk

Low profit generation / Low manufacturing(sourcing) risk

Low profit generation / High manufacturing(sourcing) risk

Q18. On a scale from one to four, with "4" being very important and "1" being unimportant,please specify the importance of the following location factors in your company's international plant location decision for the above

227

product/product line.

COST

Total Cost of Product

Participation in International Economic Trading Group

Tax Rates

Cost of Quota

Government Incentives

Cost of Land

Transaction Costs

AVAILABILITY

Availability of Transportation Modes

Availability of Middle Management

Availability of Skilled Labor

Availability of New Markets

Availability of Suppliers

Bargaining Power of Suppliers

Availability of Raw Materials

Availability of Technology

Availability of Capital

Availability of Infrastructure

Availability of Government Incentives

Availability of Lending Institutions

ACCESIBILITY

Lead Time

Proximity to Markets

Proximity of Suppliers

Flexibility of the Production

Local Integration between Fabric and Garment Manufacturers

QUALITY

Quality of the Product

Ethical Standards

Environmental Standards

RISK/

UNCERTAINTY

Labor Unions

Income Trends

Population Trends

Location of Competitors

Political Stability

Currency Stability

Banking System Stability

Interest Rate

Inflation Rate

Delivery Reliability

National Content Laws of the Countries

EASE OF OPERATIONS

Participation in International Economic Trading Group

229

Clarity of Corporate Investment Rules

Regulations concerning Joint Ventures and Mergers

Taxation of Foreign-owned Companies

Favorable Ownership Rights

Favorable Legal Systems

Favorable Import/Export Regulations

QUALITY OF LIFE

Availability of universities, colleges, schools

Cost of Living

Size of per capita income

Monthly Average Temperature

OTHER

Other

Other

Q19. Company Name :

Q20. Company Address :

Q21. Number of Employees :

Q22. Manufacturing Areas (please, select all that apply):

Fiber

Textiles

Apparel

Nonwovens

Q23. Total Sales 2001 ($ million):   100-300

   300-500

   500-700

   700-more

Q24.   R&D Percentage of Total Expenditures(%):

   0-5

   6-10

   11-15

   16 and more

Q25.   Annual Total Inventory Turnover Rate (approx.) :

(Cost of Goods Sold from Stock Sales during the Past 12 Months / Average

Inventory Investment during the Past 12 Months)

Q26. Company's On-time Delivery Percentage : %

Q27. Do your answers relate to the experience of a single plant location or

more than one location?

   Single Plant Location   More than one plant location   All of

   Company's Plants

        If more than one plant location, please indicate quantity

Q28. Your Name :

Q29. Your Position:

Q30. Years of experience in the same company :

   1-2 yrs 2-5 yrs 5-10 yrs 10 yrs and above

Q31. Do you have an active role in plant location decision making process? Yes

No

Q32. Please indicate your number of years of experience in plant location

decisions: years in this company

   years from past experience

APPENDIX C: Letters for Survey Implementation

1. Pre-notice Letter

2. Cover Letter

3. Thank-You Card

4. Replacement Cover Letter

APPENDIX C -1 Pre-notice Letter

NC STATE UNIVERSITY

College of Textiles
Department of Textiles and Apparel,
Technology and Management
Campus Box 8301, NCSU
Raleigh, NC 27695-8301
(919) 515-6449 (office)
(919) 515-3733 (fax)

July 1, 2002

Mr. ………
…………..

A few days from now you will receive a request via e-mail to complete a questionnaire for an important research project, funded by the National Textile Center (NTC). The project is a study about the managerial decision-making activities as it relates to plant location investments. The purpose of the questionnaire is to consult real world expertise in order to determine the different decision making behaviors of companies.

This advance notice is sent partly because many people would like to know ahead of time to identify the appropriate person(s) (e.g., strategic planning, logistics, marketing, etc.) those who are taking a role in plant location decision analysis.

The data collected from this questionnaire will be analyzed and used to construct and validate the international plant location decisions model. A software tool will be developed based on this model.

Given the increasing and varied levels of global competition, it is important that US textile and apparel companies have a tool to use for understanding the complex nature of decision-making for plant location as a strategy for growth. Your participation in this project will assist in the development of such a tool.

Thank you for your time and consideration.

Sincerely,

Sedef Uncu
Phd Student & Research Assistant

George L. Hodge, Ph.D.
Associate Professor and Project Director

APPENDIX C-2 Cover Letter

NC STATE UNIVERSITY

College of Textiles
Department of Textiles and Apparel,
Technology and Management
Campus Box 8301, NCSU
Raleigh, NC 27695-8301
(919) 515-6449 (office)
(919) 515-3733 (fax)

May 9, 2003

Dear Mr. ….,

As one of the primary decision makers for (company name), I would like to request your participation in a research study about plant location investments. This study is funded by the National Textile Center (NTC). Results can benefit the US Industry by providing
  o data sources for international business
  o a comprehensive "international plant location factors list" categorized according to the strategies of the US companies
  o a decision support tool, which considers both the quantitative factors and the qualitative factors (such as the strategic concerns, the operational concerns, and the environmental concerns) in international plant location decisions.

Since this scale of decision-making often involves the input of several department leaders, I also would like to request that this e-mail be forwarded to those who take a role in plant location decision analysis (e.g., strategic planning, logistics, marketing). And if you are not the best person, please forward the survey to the most appropriate person under these requirements.

Your answers will completely be **confidential**. All data will be reported in aggregate form to ensure that no individual companies will be identified. An executive summary of the survey results will be sent at no cost. If for some reason you prefer not to respond, please let us know by sending e-mail to the contact e-mail address.

Thank you very much for helping this important project.

Sincerely,

Sedef Uncu
Phd Student & Research Assistant

George L. Hodge, Ph.D.
Associate Professor and Project Director

235

APPENDIX C-3 Thank you Card

Last week a questionnaire seeking your opinions about plant location decisions was e-mailed to you.

If you have already completed the questionnaire, please accept our sincere thanks. If not, please do so at your nearest convenience. We are especially grateful for your help because it is only by asking people like you to share your experiences that we can understand how companies decide to locate their plants.

Please visit the below URL.

http://www4.ncsu.edu/~suncu/survey/

Best regards,

Sedef Uncu

APPENDIX C-4 Replacement Cover Letter

NC STATE UNIVERSITY

College of Textiles
Department of Textiles and Apparel,
Technology and Management
Campus Box 8301, NCSU
Raleigh, NC 27695-8301
(919) 515-6449 (office)
(919) 515-3733 (fax)

February 25, 2003

Dear ....,

About three weeks ago I sent a questionnaire to you that asked about your participation in a research study about plant location investments. To the best of my knowledge it is not yet been submitted.

The comments of people who have already responded include a wide variety of differences in plant location investments. Many have described their experience in trying to find the right country to invest. I think the aggregated results are going to be very useful to all of the US textile and apparel companies in this global environment.

We are writing again because of the importance of your responses in arriving at meaningful conclusions. It is only by hearing from nearly everyone in the sample that we can be sure that the results are truly representative.

A few people have responded to say that they could not open the website or could not submit the information. If this is the case for your company, please send me your fax number so that I can fax you a written copy of my survey.

Your answers will completely be **confidential**. All data will be reported in aggregate form to ensure that no individual companies will be identified.

We hope that you will fill out and return the questionnaire soon. If for any reason you prefer not to respond, please let us know by sending e-mail to the contact e-mail address.

Thank you very much for helping this important project. *You can enter the survey by clicking the below URL.*

http://www4.ncsu.edu/~suncu/survey/

Sincerely,

Sedef Uncu
Phd Student & Research Assistant

George L. Hodge, Ph.D.
Associate Professor and Project Director

APPENDIX D: Results of Survey – Listed According to Corporate
Strategy

Corporate Strategy

COST

COST LEADERSHIP	Total Cost of Product	Particiaption in Trade Groups	Tax	Quota Cost	Government Incentives	Land Cost	Transaction Cost
Mean	4.00	2.83	2.83	2.17	3.00	3.17	3.00
Median	4.00	3.00	2.50	2.00	3.00	3.00	3.50
Mode	4.00	3.00	2.00	1.00	3.00	3.00	4.00
Range	0.00	3.00	2.00	3.00	2.00	2.00	3.00
Minimum	4.00	1.00	2.00	1.00	2.00	2.00	1.00
Maximum	4.00	4.00	4.00	4.00	4.00	4.00	4.00
Sum	24.00	17.00	17.00	13.00	18.00	19.00	18.00
Count (n)	6.00	6.00	6.00	6.00	6.00	6.00	6.00

DIFFERENTIATION	Total Cost of Product	Particiaption in trade groups	Tax	Quota Cost	Government Incentives	Land Cost	Transaction Cost
Mean	4.00	2.43	2.86	3.43	3.14	2.71	2.86
Median	4.00	2.00	3.00	3.00	3.00	3.00	3.00
Mode	4.00	2.00	3.00	3.00	3.00	3.00	3.00
Range	0.00	3.00	3.00	1.00	1.00	2.00	1.00
Minimum	4.00	1.00	1.00	3.00	3.00	1.00	2.00
Maximum	4.00	4.00	4.00	4.00	4.00	3.00	3.00
Sum	28.00	17.00	20.00	24.00	22.00	19.00	20.00
Count (n)	7.00	7.00	7.00	7.00	7.00	7.00	7.00

FOCUS	Total Cost of Product	Particiaption in trade groups	Tax	Quota Cost	Government Incentives	Land Cost	Transaction Cost
Mean	3.50	2.25	2.75	2.75	3.00	3.25	3.00
Median	3.50	2.50	2.50	3.00	3.00	3.50	3.00
Mode	3.00	3.00	2.00	3.00	2.00	4.00	#N/A
Range	1.00	2.00	2.00	3.00	2.00	2.00	2.00
Minimum	3.00	1.00	2.00	1.00	2.00	2.00	2.00
Maximum	4.00	3.00	4.00	4.00	4.00	4.00	4.00
Sum	14.00	9.00	11.00	11.00	12.00	13.00	9.00
Count (n)	4.00	4.00	4.00	4.00	4.00	4.00	3.00

Ranking on a scale of 1 to 4, 1 being unimportant, 4 being most important

Similar statistics were compiled for the rest of the categories.

APPENDIX E: Results of Survey – Listed According to Growth Strategy

Growth Strategy

COST

GREENFIELD OPERATIONS	Total Cost of Product	Participation in Trade Groups	Tax	Quota Cost	Government Incentives	Land Cost	Transaction Cost
Mean	3.78	2.67	2.89	2.56	3.00	3.22	2.88
Median	4.00	3.00	3.00	3.00	3.00	3.00	3.00
Mode	4.00	3.00	2.00	3.00	4.00	3.00	3.00
Range	1.00	3.00	2.00	3.00	2.00	2.00	3.00
Minimum	3.00	1.00	2.00	1.00	2.00	2.00	1.00
Maximum	4.00	4.00	4.00	4.00	4.00	4.00	4.00
Sum	34.00	24.00	26.00	23.00	27.00	29.00	23.00
Count (n)	9.00	9.00	9.00	9.00	9.00	9.00	8.00

Ranking on a scale of 1 to 4, 1 being unimportant, 4 being most important

STRATEGIC PARTNERSHIPS	Total Cost of Product	Participation in Trade Groups	Tax	Quota Cost	Government Incentives	Land Cost	Transaction Cost
Mean	3.85	2.69	3.15	2.85	3.00	3.00	3.08
Median	4.00	3.00	3.00	3.00	3.00	3.00	3.00
Mode	4.00	3.00	4.00	3.00	3.00	3.00	3.00
Range	1.00	3.00	2.00	3.00	2.00	2.00	2.00
Minimum	3.00	1.00	2.00	1.00	2.00	2.00	2.00
Maximum	4.00	4.00	4.00	4.00	4.00	4.00	4.00
Sum	50.00	35.00	41.00	37.00	39.00	39.00	37.00
Count (n)	13.00	13.00	13.00	13.00	13.00	13.00	12.00

Ranking on a scale of 1 to 4, 1 being unimportant, 4 being most important

SOURCING	Total Cost of Product	Participation in Trade Groups	Tax	Quota Cost	Government Incentives	Land Cost	Transaction Cost
Mean	3.92	2.38	2.92	3.08	3.15	2.85	3.00
Median	4.00	2.00	3.00	3.00	3.00	3.00	3.00
Mode	4.00	2.00	3.00	3.00	3.00	3.00	3.00
Range	1.00	3.00	3.00	3.00	2.00	3.00	2.00
Minimum	3.00	1.00	1.00	1.00	2.00	1.00	2.00
Maximum	4.00	4.00	4.00	4.00	4.00	4.00	4.00
Sum	51.00	31.00	38.00	40.00	41.00	37.00	36.00
Count (n)	13.00	13.00	13.00	13.00	13.00	13.00	12.00

Ranking on a scale of 1 to 4, 1 being unimportant, 4 being most important

Similar statistics were compiled for the rest of the categories.

APPENDIX F: Results of Survey – Listed According to Product Strategy

Product Strategy

COST

HIGH PROFIT / HIGH RISK	Total Cost of Product	Participation in Trade Groups	Tax	Quota Cost	Government Incentives	Land Cost	Transaction Cost
Mean (High Profit/High Risk)	3.60	2.80	2.60	2.40	2.40	2.60	2.60
Median	4.00	3.00	2.00	3.00	2.00	3.00	3.00
Mode	4.00	2.00	2.00	3.00	2.00	3.00	3.00
Range	1.00	2.00	2.00	3.00	1.00	1.00	1.00
Minimum	3.00	2.00	2.00	1.00	2.00	2.00	2.00
Maximum	4.00	4.00	4.00	4.00	3.00	3.00	3.00
Sum	18.00	14.00	13.00	12.00	12.00	13.00	13.00
Count (n)	5.00	5.00	5.00	5.00	5.00	5.00	5.00

Ranking on a scale of 1 to 4, 1 being unimportant, 4 being most important

HIGH PROFIT / LOW RISK	Total Cost of Product	Participation in Trade Groups	Tax	Quota Cost	Government Incentives	Land Cost	Transaction Cost
Mean (High Profit/Low Risk)	4.00	2.67	2.83	3.00	3.00	2.67	2.83
Median	4.00	2.50	3.00	3.00	3.00	3.00	3.00
Mode	4.00	2.00	4.00	3.00	3.00	3.00	3.00
Range	0.00	3.00	3.00	3.00	2.00	2.00	1.00
Minimum	4.00	1.00	1.00	1.00	2.00	1.00	2.00
Maximum	4.00	4.00	4.00	4.00	4.00	3.00	3.00
Sum	24.00	16.00	17.00	18.00	18.00	16.00	17.00
Count (n)	6.00	6.00	6.00	6.00	6.00	6.00	6.00

Ranking on a scale of 1 to 4, 1 being unimportant, 4 being most important

LOW PROFIT / LOW RISK	Total Cost of Product	Participation in Trade Groups	Tax	Quota Cost	Government Incentives	Land Cost	Transaction Cost
Mean (Low Profit/Low Risk)	4.00	2.00	2.80	2.80	3.60	3.60	3.40
Median	4.00	2.00	3.00	3.00	4.00	4.00	4.00
Mode	4.00	3.00	2.00	3.00	4.00	4.00	4.00
Range	0.00	2.00	2.00	3.00	1.00	1.00	3.00
Minimum	4.00	1.00	2.00	1.00	3.00	3.00	1.00
Maximum	4.00	3.00	4.00	4.00	4.00	4.00	4.00
Sum	20.00	10.00	14.00	14.00	18.00	18.00	17.00
Count (n)	5.00	5.00	5.00	5.00	5.00	5.00	5.00

Ranking on a scale of 1 to 4, 1 being unimportant, 4 being most important

LOW PROFIT / HIGH RISK	Total Cost of Product	Participation in Trade Groups	Tax	Quota Cost	Government Incentives	Land Cost	Transaction Cost
Mean (Low Profit/High Risk)	4.00	3.00	4.00	4.00	4.00	4.00	

Ranking on a scale of 1 to 4, 1 being unimportant, 4 being most important

Similar statistics were compiled for the rest of the categories.

APPENDIX G: Results of Survey – Listed According to Operational
Strategy

Operational Strategy

COST

INNOVATION	Total Cost of Product	Participation in Trade Groups	Tax	Quota Cost	Government Incentives	Land Cost	Transaction Cost
Mean	3.83	2.75	2.83	2.83	3.00	3.00	2.73
Median	4.00	3.00	3.00	3.00	3.00	3.00	3.00
Mode	4.00	2.00	4.00	3.00	3.00	3.00	3.00
Range	1.00	2.00	3.00	3.00	2.00	3.00	3.00
Minimum	3.00	2.00	1.00	1.00	2.00	1.00	1.00
Maximum	4.00	4.00	4.00	4.00	4.00	4.00	4.00
Sum	46.00	33.00	34.00	34.00	36.00	36.00	30.00
Count (n)	12.00	12.00	12.00	12.00	12.00	12.00	11.00

Ranking on a scale of 1 to 4, 1 being unimportant, 4 being most important

QUALITY	Total Cost of Product	Participation in Trade Groups	Tax	Quota Cost	Government Incentives	Land Cost	Transaction Cost
Mean	3.88	2.63	2.75	2.75	3.00	3.00	2.87
Median	4.00	3.00	3.00	3.00	3.00	3.00	3.00
Mode	4.00	3.00	2.00	3.00	3.00	3.00	3.00
Range	1.00	3.00	3.00	3.00	2.00	3.00	3.00
Minimum	3.00	1.00	1.00	1.00	2.00	1.00	1.00
Maximum	4.00	4.00	4.00	4.00	4.00	4.00	4.00
Sum	62.00	42.00	44.00	44.00	48.00	48.00	43.00
Count (n)	16.00	16.00	16.00	16.00	16.00	16.00	15.00

Ranking on a scale of 1 to 4, 1 being unimportant, 4 being most important

CONTINUOUS IMPROVEMENT	Total Cost of Product	Participation in Trade Groups	Tax	Quota Cost	Government Incentives	Land Cost	Transaction Cost
Mean	3.92	2.67	2.92	3.00	3.00	2.92	3.00
Median	4.00	3.00	3.00	3.00	3.00	3.00	3.00
Mode	4.00	3.00	4.00	3.00	3.00	3.00	3.00
Range	1.00	3.00	3.00	3.00	2.00	3.00	2.00
Minimum	3.00	1.00	1.00	1.00	2.00	1.00	2.00
Maximum	4.00	4.00	4.00	4.00	4.00	4.00	4.00
Sum	47.00	32.00	35.00	36.00	36.00	35.00	33.00
Count (n)	12.00	12.00	12.00	12.00	12.00	12.00	11.00

Ranking on a scale of 1 to 4, 1 being unimportant, 4 being most important

SPEED	Total Cost of Product	Participation in Trade Groups	Tax	Quota Cost	Government Incentives	Land Cost	Transaction Cost
Mean	3.91	2.73	2.91	2.82	2.91	2.73	2.80
Median	4.00	3.00	3.00	3.00	3.00	3.00	3.00
Mode	4.00	2.00	4.00	4.00	3.00	3.00	3.00
Range	1.00	3.00	3.00	3.00	2.00	3.00	2.00
Minimum	3.00	1.00	1.00	1.00	2.00	1.00	2.00
Maximum	4.00	4.00	4.00	4.00	4.00	4.00	4.00
Sum	43.00	30.00	32.00	31.00	32.00	30.00	28.00
Count (n)	11.00	11.00	11.00	11.00	11.00	11.00	10.00

Ranking on a scale of 1 to 4, 1 being unimportant, 4 being most important

FLEXIBILITY	Total Cost of Product	Participation in Trade Groups	Tax	Quota Cost	Government Incentives	Land Cost	Transaction Cost
Mean	3.91	2.82	3.00	3.00	3.00	2.91	3.00
Median	4.00	3.00	3.00	3.00	3.00	3.00	3.00
Mode	4.00	3.00	4.00	3.00	3.00	3.00	3.00
Range	1.00	3.00	3.00	3.00	2.00	3.00	2.00
Minimum	3.00	1.00	1.00	1.00	2.00	1.00	2.00
Maximum	4.00	4.00	4.00	4.00	4.00	4.00	4.00
Sum	43.00	31.00	33.00	33.00	33.00	32.00	30.00
Count (n)	11.00	11.00	11.00	11.00	11.00	11.00	10.00

Ranking on a scale of 1 to 4, 1 being unimportant, 4 being most important

Similar statistics were compiled for the rest of the categories.

APPENDIX H: Results of Survey – Listed According to Level of Risk
Taking

Risk Type

COST

MEDIUM RISK	Total Cost of Product	Participation in Trade Groups	Tax	Quota Cost	Government Incentives	Land Cost	Transaction Cost
Mean	3.90	3.00	3.00	2.40	3.00	3.00	2.67
Median	4.00	3.00	3.00	3.00	3.00	3.00	3.00
Mode	4.00	3.00	3.00	3.00	3.00	3.00	3.00
Range	1.00	2.00	2.00	3.00	2.00	2.00	3.00
Minimum	3.00	2.00	2.00	1.00	2.00	2.00	1.00
Maximum	4.00	4.00	4.00	4.00	4.00	4.00	4.00
Sum	39.00	30.00	30.00	24.00	30.00	30.00	24.00
Count (n)	10.00	10.00	10.00	10.00	10.00	10.00	9.00

Ranking on a scale of 1 to 4, 1 being unimportant, 4 being most important

LOW RISK	Total Cost of Product	Participation in Trade Groups	Tax	Quota Cost	Government Incentives	Land Cost	Transaction Cost
Mean	3.83	1.67	2.67	3.50	3.17	2.83	3.17
Median	4.00	1.50	2.50	3.50	3.00	3.00	3.00
Mode	4.00	1.00	2.00	4.00	3.00	3.00	3.00
Range	1.00	2.00	3.00	1.00	2.00	3.00	2.00
Minimum	3.00	1.00	1.00	3.00	2.00	1.00	2.00
Maximum	4.00	3.00	4.00	4.00	4.00	4.00	4.00
Sum	23.00	10.00	16.00	21.00	19.00	17.00	19.00
Count (n)	6.00	6.00	6.00	6.00	6.00	6.00	6.00

Ranking on a scale of 1 to 4, 1 being unimportant, 4 being most important

AVAILABILITY

MEDIUM RISK	Transportation	Middle Management	Skilled Labor	New Markets	Suppliers	Bargaining power of suppliers
Mean	3.80	3.40	3.40	3.10	3.60	2.80
Median	4.00	3.50	3.00	3.50	4.00	3.00
Mode	4.00	4.00	3.00	4.00	4.00	3.00
Range	1.00	2.00	1.00	3.00	1.00	3.00
Minimum	3.00	2.00	3.00	1.00	3.00	1.00
Maximum	4.00	4.00	4.00	4.00	4.00	4.00
Sum	38.00	34.00	34.00	31.00	36.00	28.00
Count (n)	10.00	10.00	10.00	10.00	10.00	10.00

	Raw Materials	Technology	Capital	Infrastructure	Availability of incentives	Lending institutions
Mean	3.40	3.00	3.50	3.60	3.00	2.70
Median	3.50	3.00	3.50	4.00	3.00	3.00
Mode	4.00	3.00	4.00	4.00	3.00	3.00
Range	2.00	3.00	1.00	1.00	2.00	1.00
Minimum	2.00	1.00	3.00	3.00	2.00	2.00
Maximum	4.00	4.00	4.00	4.00	4.00	3.00
Sum	34.00	30.00	35.00	36.00	30.00	27.00
Count (n)	10.00	10.00	10.00	10.00	10.00	10.00

Ranking on a scale of 1 to 4, 1 being unimportant, 4 being most important

Similar statistics were compiled for the rest of the categories.

APPENDIX I: Results of Survey – Listed According to Sector Type

Sector Type

COST

FIBER	Total Cost of Product	Participation in Trade Groups	Tax	Quota Cost	Government Incentives	Land Cost	Transaction Cost
Mean	4.00	3.00	3.50	3.50	3.50	3.50	3.00
Median	4.00	3.00	3.50	3.50	3.50	3.50	3.00
Mode	4.00	3.00	#N/A	#N/A	#N/A	#N/A	#N/A
Range	0.00	0.00	1.00	1.00	1.00	1.00	0.00
Minimum	4.00	3.00	3.00	3.00	3.00	3.00	3.00
Maximum	4.00	3.00	4.00	4.00	4.00	4.00	3.00
Sum	8.00	6.00	7.00	7.00	7.00	7.00	3.00
Count (n)	2.00	2.00	2.00	2.00	2.00	2.00	1.00

Ranking on a scale of 1 to 4, 1 being unimportant, 4 being most important

TEXTILES	Total Cost of Product	Participation in Trade Groups	Tax	Quota Cost	Government Incentives	Land Cost	Transaction Cost
Mean	3.90	2.80	2.80	2.30	3.00	3.20	2.89
Median	4.00	3.00	3.00	3.00	3.00	3.00	3.00
Mode	4.00	3.00	3.00	3.00	3.00	3.00	4.00
Range	1.00	3.00	2.00	3.00	2.00	2.00	3.00
Minimum	3.00	1.00	2.00	1.00	2.00	2.00	1.00
Maximum	4.00	4.00	4.00	4.00	4.00	4.00	4.00
Sum	39.00	28.00	28.00	23.00	30.00	32.00	26.00
Count (n)	10.00	10.00	10.00	10.00	10.00	10.00	9.00

Ranking on a scale of 1 to 4, 1 being unimportant, 4 being most important

APPAREL	Total Cost of Product	Participation in Trade Groups	Tax	Quota Cost	Government Incentives	Land Cost	Transaction Cost
Mean	3.86	2.00	2.86	3.29	3.14	2.57	2.86
Median	4.00	2.00	3.00	4.00	3.00	3.00	3.00
Mode	4.00	2.00	4.00	4.00	3.00	3.00	3.00
Range	1.00	3.00	3.00	3.00	2.00	2.00	2.00
Minimum	3.00	1.00	1.00	1.00	2.00	1.00	2.00
Maximum	4.00	4.00	4.00	4.00	4.00	3.00	4.00
Sum	27.00	14.00	20.00	23.00	22.00	18.00	20.00
Count (n)	7.00	7.00	7.00	7.00	7.00	7.00	7.00

Ranking on a scale of 1 to 4, 1 being unimportant, 4 being most important

NONWOVENS	Total Cost of Product	Participation in Trade Groups	Tax	Quota Cost	Government Incentives	Land Cost	Transaction Cost
Mean	3.50	3.50	2.50	3.00	2.50	3.00	3.00
Median	3.50	3.50	2.50	3.00	2.50	3.00	3.00
Mode	#N/A	#N/A	#N/A	3.00	#N/A	3.00	3.00
Range	1.00	1.00	1.00	0.00	1.00	0.00	0.00
Minimum	3.00	3.00	2.00	3.00	2.00	3.00	3.00
Maximum	4.00	4.00	3.00	3.00	3.00	3.00	3.00
Sum	7.00	7.00	5.00	6.00	5.00	6.00	6.00
Count (n)	2.00	2.00	2.00	2.00	2.00	2.00	2.00

Ranking on a scale of 1 to 4, 1 being unimportant, 4 being most important

Similar statistics were compiled for the rest of the categories.

APPENDIX J: Economic Agencies

Source: http://www.siteselection.com

Location	Company	Contact	Phone	URL
Buenos Aires, ARGENTINA	Secretariat of Industry & Commerce	Debora Giorgi, Secretary	54-1-349-3406	www.presidencia.gov.ar/
Canberra, ACT AUSTRALIA	Department of Trade	Mark Vaile, Minister	61-6-277-7420	www.dca.gov.au
Nassau, BAHAMAS	Ministry of Finance, Planning & Econ. Dev.	William Allen, Minister	1-242-327-1530	http:///
Brussels, BELGIUM	Ministry of Foreign Affairs, Foreign Trade & Development Aid	Louis Michel, Minister	32-2-516-8111	http://diplobel.fgov.be
Brasilia, BRAZIL	Ministry of Industry, Commerce & Tourism	Sergio Amaral, Minister	55-61-225-8105	www.mdic.gov.br
Bandar Seri Begawan, BRUNEI	Ministry of Development	Dr. Haji Ismail bin Pengiran Haji Damit, Minister	673-2-383911	http:///
Santiago, CHILE	Ministry of Economy, Mining & Energy	Jorge Rodriguez Grossi, Minister	56-2-672-5522	www.economia.cl
Beijing, CHINA	Ministry of Foreign Econ. Relations & Trade	Shi Guangsheng, Minister	86-10-6512-6644	www.moftec.gov.cn/
San Jose, COSTA RICA	Ministry of Economy and Industries	Gilberto Barrantes, Minister	506-235-2700	www.meic.go.cr
Havana, CUBA	Ministry of Foreign Investment & Econ. Corp.	Marta Lomas Morales, Minister	53-7-33-3110	http:///
Copenhagen, DENMARK	Ministry of Business and Industry	Pia Gjellerup, Minister	45-33-92-33-50	www.em.dk/
Santo Domingo, DOMINICAN REPUBLIC	Secretariat of Industry & Commerce	Hugo Guiliani Cury, Secretary of State	1-809-685-5171	http:///
Cairo, EGYPT	Ministry of Economy	Dr. Youssef Boutros-Ghali, Minister	20-2-3916802	http:///
Helsinki, FINLAND	Ministry of Trade & Industry	Sinikka Monkare, Minister	358-9-1601	www.vn.fi/ktm/
Paris, FRANCE	Ministry of Economy, Finance & Industry	Laurent Fabius, Minister	33-1-40-04-04-04	www.finances.gouv.fr
Berlin, GERMANY	Federal Ministry of Econ. Cooperation & Dev.	Heidermarie Wieczorek, Federal Minister	49-228-5350	www.bmwi.de/
Athens, GREECE	Ministry of Development	Nikos Christodoulakis, Minister	30-1-748-2770	www.ypan.gr/
Tamuning, GUAM	Guam Econ. Dev. Authority	Ed Untalan, Administrator	671-647-4332	www.investGuam.com
Hong Kong, HONG KONG	Government Secretariat	Sandra Lee, Secretary Econ. Services	852-2810-2717	www.info.gov.hk
Budapest, HUNGARY	Ministry of Economic Affairs	Gyorgy Matolcsi, Minister	36-1-302-2355	www.gm.hu/
New Delhi, INDIA	Ministry of Commerce & Industry	Murasoli Maran, Minister	91-11-3015299	www.commin.nic.in/
Jakarta Selatan, INDONESIA	Department of Industry & Trade	Gen. (Ret.) Luhut Panjaithan, Minister	62-21-5256458	http://indag.dprin.go.id/
Dublin, IRELAND	Department of Enterprise, Trade & Employment	Mary Harney, Minister	353-1-6614444	www.irlgov.ie/entemp/
Jerusalem, ISRAEL	Ministry of Industry & Trade	Dalya Itzik, Minister	972-2-622-0200	www.israel-industry-trade.gov.il/
Rome, ITALY	Ministry of Finance & Economy	Giulio Tremonti, Minister	39-06-59971	www.finanze.it/
Kingston, JAMACIA	Ministry of Industry & Investments	Phillip Paulwell, Minister	1-876-929-8990	http:///
Tokyo, JAPAN	Ministry of Int'l Trade, Industry & Economy	Takeo Hiranuma, Minister	81-3-3501-1511	www.miti.go.jp/

Location	Ministry	Contact	Phone	Website
Luxembourg, LUXEMBOURG	Ministry of Economy & Trade	Henri Grethen, Minister	352-478-4106	www.etat.lu/ECO/
Kuala Lumpur, MALAYSIA	Ministry of Int'l Trade & Industry	Paduka Rafidah Azia, Minister	60-3-2540033	http://miti.gov.my/
Mexico D.F., MEXICO	Secretariat of Economy	Luis Ernesto Derbez, Secretary	52-5-286-1823	www.secofi-siem.gob.mx
Rabat, MOROCCO	Ministry of Finance & Economy	Fatallah Oualalou, Minister	212-7-76-31-71	www.mfie.gov.ma/
The Hague, NETHERLANDS	Ministry of Economic Affairs & Foreign Trade	Annemarie Jorritsma, Minister	31-70-379-8911	http://info.minez.nl/
Wellington, NEW ZEALAND	Department of Commerce	Paul Swain, Minister	64-4-474-2930	www.moc.govt.nz/
Abuja Federal Capital Teritory, NIGERIA	Ministry of Industry	Chief Kola Jamodu, Minister	234-9-234-3293	http:///
Oslo, NORWAY	Ministry of Trade & Industry	Olav Akselsen, Minister	47-22-24-90-90	http://odin.dep.no/nhd/
Islamabad, PAKISTAN	Ministry of Commerce, Industry & Production	Abdul Razzak Daud, Minister	92-51-924548	http://alephx.org/paktrade/
Metro Manila, PHILIPPINES	National Economic Dev. Authority (NEDA)	Ruperto Alonzo, Depty. Dir. General, National Dev.	63-2-631-0945	www.neda.gov.ph/
Warsaw, POLAND	Ministry of Economic Affairs	Jacek Piechota, Minister	48-22-693-50-00	http:///
Lisbon, PORTUGAL	Ministry of Economic Affairs	Luis Braga da Cruz, Minister	351-1-3228600	www.min-economia.pt
Moscow, RUSSIA	Ministry of Economic Dev. & Trade	German Gref, Minister	7-095-203-63-10	http:///
Riyadh, SAUDI ARABIA	Ministry of Commerce	Osama bin Jaafer Faqih, Minister	966-1-401-2220	http:///
Singapore, SINGAPORE	Ministry of Trade & Industry	Brig. Gen. George Yong-Boon Yeo, Minister	65-2259911	www.mti.gov.sg/
Pretoria, SOUTH AFRICA	Ministry of Trade & Industry	Alex Erwin, Minister	27-12-322-7677	www.dti.pwv.gov.za
Kwachon, Kyonggi, SOUTH KOREA	Ministry of Trade, Industry & Energy	Chang Che Shik, Minister	82-2-503-9404	www.mocie.go.kr/
Madrid, SPAIN	Ministry of Economy	Rodrigo Rato y Figaredo, Minister	34-91-595-8000	www.mineco.es//
Stockholm, SWEDEN	Ministry of Industry & Commerce	Bjorn Rosengren, Minister	46-8-405-10-00	www.naring.regeringen.se/
Bern, SWIZTERLAND	Federal Dept. of Econ. Affairs	Pascal Couchepin, Chief	41-31-322-21-11	www.evd.admin.ch
Taipei, TAIWAN	Ministry of Econ. Affairs	Lin Hsin-I, Minister	886-2-2321-2200	www.moea.gov.tw/
Bangkok, THAILAND	Ministry of Industry	Suriya Chungrungruangkit, Minister	66-2-202-3000	www.industry.go.th/
Port of Spain, TRINIDAD & TOBAGO	Ministry of Trade & Industry	Mervyn Assam, Minister	1-868-623-2931	http:///
Tunis, TUNISIA	Ministry of Econ. Dev.	Abdel Atif Saddam, Minister	216-1-334-022	http:///
Ankara, TURKEY	Ministry of Industry & Commerce	Ahmet Kenan Tanrikulu, Minister	90-312-231-4866	www.sanayi.gov.tr/
Abu Dhabi, UNITED ARAB EMIRATES	Ministry of Economy & Commerce	Sheikh Fahim bin Sultan al-Qassimi, Minister	971-2-336954	www.economy.gov.ae/
London, UNITED KINGDOM	Dept. of Trade & Industry	Patricia Hewitt, Secy. Of State & Pres. Of Board of Trade.	44-020-7215-5000	www.dti.gov.uk/
Caracas, VENEZUELA	Ministry of Industry & Commerce	Luisa Romero Bermudez, Minister	58-2-731-3027	http:///